My solution to America's problems is the kitchen table.

GT

PUBLISHING
NEW YORK

Naomi's
HOME COMPANION

A Treasury of

Favorite Recipes,

Food for Thought,

and Kitchen

Wit and Wisdom

N A O M I   J U D D

Editorial Development—David Ricketts   Art Direction and Design—Barbara Marks

Produced by David Ricketts and Barbara Marks

David Ricketts, *Editorial Development*

Barbara Marks, *Art Direction and Design*

Beth Mackin, *Production Director*

Recipe Testers:

JoAnn Brett

Maureen Luchejko

Frank Melodia

Paul Piccuito

Sarah Reynolds

Steven Mark Needham, *Food Photographer*

Anne Disrude, *Food Stylist*

Michael Pederson, *Food Stylist Assistant*

Betty Alfenito, *Prop Stylist*

Denise Canter, *Prop Stylist*

Location Photography:

Chip Powell, *Photographer*

Elise Walker, *Food Stylist*

Pam Mayberry, *Food Stylist Assistant*

Holly Klein, *Prop Stylist*

CJ Pyles, *Prop Stylist Assistant*

Stephen Frankel, *Copy Editor and Proofreader*

Jessica Cunningham, *Proofreader*

Cover:

Chip Powell, *Photographer*

David Ballard, *Naomi Judd's Hair*

Marina Torpin, *Naomi Judd's Makeup*

Laurie Kelley, *Naomi Judd's Personal Assistant*

Produced by David Ricketts and Barbara Marks

Food photography by Steven Mark Needham © 1997

Additional acknowledgments and picture credits are on page 211.

Published in 1997 by GT Publishing Corporation

16 East 40th Street, New York, NY 10016

Library of Congress Cataloging-in-Publication Data

Judd, Naomi.
        Naomi's home companion : a treasury of favorite recipes, food for thought, and kitchen wit and wisdom / Naomi Judd.
              p.   cm.
        Includes index.
        ISBN 1-57719-271-0 (hardcover)
        1. Cookery, American.   2. Country musicians—Social life and customs.
        3. Judd, Naomi—Biography.   I. Title.
        TX715.J9   1997
        641.5973—dc21   97-30260
                                                                                                             CIP

ISBN: 1-57719-271-0

Printed in Singapore

2 4 6 8 10 9 7 5 3 1

First Printing

Acknowledgments

Pete Coors, the CEO of Coors Bottling Co., told me something very sobering: "When you find a turtle up on a fence post, you know he had some help getting up there."

So thanks to the folks who put me up to this:

Muchas gracias to the folks at GoodTimes Publishing who saw El Photo Grande: *Tom Klusaritz,* Vice President of Publishing, *Andy Greenberg,* President GT Entertainment, and *Lynn Hamlin,* Senior Vice President GT Direct.

David Ricketts, our editor, who played Ethel to my Lucy, was as patient as Job on this job, while keeping readers from thinking I'm totally whacked. Also to *Barbara Marks* who goes with David like Beans and Franks and shares her outstanding artistic talents with us.

My publicist *Kathy Allmand* from Front Page Publicity for proofing and polishing.

"The Suits" who sit behind desks while I'm in my own kitchen or eating in the restaurants of America: *Rick ("Jerry McGuire") Bradley* and *Rick Hersh* at the William Morris Agency.

My manager and husband *Larry Strickland* who advised me to turn down Playboy and then asks, "What's for supper, honey?"

And to the rest of my family who keeps our kitchen humming with love, laughter, and learning, especially *Sweet Pea* and *Sweet Tater,* who put the spice in my life.

Finally, I echo the acceptance speech of Maureen Stapleton, when she won the Oscar for Best Supporting Actress: "I'd like to thank everyone I ever met."

*I dedicate this book
to my Mom,
Pauline Ruth Judd Rideout,
and to her Grandmother,
Cora Lee Burton,
the two matriarchs who ruled
from their kitchen kingdoms.*

Foreword

elcome—c'mon in, pull up a chair, and put on your bib and your thinkin' cap. I hope you have an appetite for fun. In my kitchen we use Shake 'n' Giggles and Humor Helper.

This is a how-to book with recipes to fix fine food and fill up bellies as well as recipes for new ways to think. There are tips on how to raise kids without Ritalin® or chloroform and on how to get your casserole dishes returned. What to do if you find a Band-Aid in your soup? Does possum really taste like chicken? How to trap your own mongoose. How to improve your sex life and get your kids off smack, crack, and pot. Discover what moderate Republicans have hidden in their pantry. See what's behind butt-extender food. Learn the difference between jam and jelly and why jam don't shake. Get the scoop on the latest in hairnet fashions. Learn how to eat an entire turkey without using your hands.

Find out what really goes on behind the walls of the Judd house. Read about what makes one Judd gag, how another rigs a race, and which ones went public as the letter Y. Get the scoop on Judd secret codes and rituals. Come along as we unravel the unsolved mystery of who left the cap off the CheezWhiz and uncover the shocking truth about those Keebler Elves and the real tragedy behind freezer burn. See in black and white why I'm called the goofiest woman in country music.

Now I'm not an expert—okay, maybe at making mistakes. But after all, an expert's just somebody from out of town with slides. I go out of town a lot, but all I have are recipes for living.

Wynonna, Ashley, Larry, and I are certainly not the perfect family. We don't do Ozzie and Harriet at our house. We're an example of real life with all its struggles, defects, and unpredictability. People say I'm the girl next door. Maybe. But I've also been around the world. I've seen that America's hungry for moral nutrition and spiritual sustenance, so I'm offering some food for thought.

We all live in a family-unfriendly culture. With the increasing power and influence of the mass media, our society really has become Hollywood versus America. Don't want to spoil your appetite, but the collapse of a nation begins in every home. Chew on that a while!

When I first heard the saying "It takes a village to raise a child," I misunderstood and heard it as "It takes the Village People to raise a child." Parents really need the community to reinforce the values they try to teach their kids in the home.

Journalist Bill Moyers told me one night at dinner, "Our children are being raised by appliances." There's no doubt TV teaches us values every bit as much as churches. Unfortunately, those TV values are not good. And my second problem about TV is that while you're spending so much of your precious life watching someone else's, you're missing out on your own. The most educational channel is called "off." This book will show you how to make the most out of your own family sitcom and how to survive real life drama.

Pardon my name-dropping throughout the book, but these folks are actually my friends and experience the same things as you and I. You'll hear about Michael Bolton removing his clothes in front of me; why actor Matthew McConaughey slept in my barn; what goes on in Tammy Wynette's bus late at night; Faith Hill's double dare in front of 25,000 people; and Jay Leno's joining the Gay Pride Parade. You're also mentioned somewhere in this book, but for the life of me I can't remember what page. Guess you'll have to read the whole darn thing.

I do hope after you read this book, your mind will be like the elastic waistband in these old p.j.s I'm wearing—stretched and unable to go back to its original size. Writing this has been as uplifting as my Wonderbra®. The voices inside my head that commanded me to write are quiet now, so I'm headed off for a month's vacation at Julia Child State Park.

With all good wishes as big as your refrigerator,

Naomi

NAOMI JUDD

Contents

These are my reasons to cook:

Love,

nutrition,

tradition,

and

celebration

• **The Family Powwow**   • **Food for Our Family**   • **It Can Only Get Better: Comfort Food**

*O*nly a few hours ago my family was gathered around our kitchen table where I now sit writing these words. We call it our Powwow. While we enjoyed the great-tasting, nourishing food, we laughed and connected with each other. It was a straightforward, homemade meal, accompanied by honest plain talk. I'll never rival Martha Stewart—we don't do fancy at our house—or be mistaken for June Cleaver. But everyone here tonight felt satisfied, secure, and valued. It was a wonderful ending to our busy day.

I love this country so much and am deeply troubled by what I see firsthand when I am away from home, traveling border to border and coast to coast doing speaking engagements. We're losing the war on crime, drugs, racism, hunger, and poverty.

My grandson Elijah Judd Kelly, age eleven months, in his high chair

I'm a pretty simple, practical person. I'm always looking for the obvious solution. I believe we have one right under our nose. It's the kitchen table. I'm convinced the answer to our social ills isn't the electric chair, it's the high chair.

We get our "first taste" of the outside world in our home. The family is a microcosm of society. The first experiences we have form our self-image and can give us self-confidence. We learn to feel loved and worthy, or otherwise. Our deepest beliefs and expectations of ourselves and others will determine how we perceive all external reality—life around us. These earliest interactions with family will then have the most profound effect on the kind of people and situations we are drawn to for the rest of our life.

When U.S. Olympic Gold Medal figure skater Scott Hamilton was asked which jump in ice skating is the hardest, he replied, "The one right after you fall!" Behavioral therapists tell us by the time a child is three years old, he or she has formed a concept of self. They see themselves as a winner or loser.

Our parents are our earliest culture leaders. From the beginning, it matters more who's the head of the family than the head of the country. Mothers teach more fundamental lessons than teachers. The Supreme Court can't legislate morality; we should see it acted out every day in our homes. The old adage "The hand that rocks the cradle rules the world" is absolutely true.

Parents and family members have a responsibility to help every child form a positive self-image and to continually reinforce self-confidence throughout his or her life.

Larry's birthday dinner at Wy's home (from left):
Larry, Ashley holding Grace, me, Wy, and her husband Arch holding Elijah

THE FAMILY POWWOW

The kitchen table was the hub of our world growing up and my Mom was always at home. Over my first eighteen years in Ashland, Kentucky, I can only count four times when I came in from school and she wasn't waiting for me. Mom would say from time to time, "Let the men run around trying to change the world. I just want to improve my own family."

Our primitive ancestors gathered around a fire 200,000 years ago. Since we now have stoves, today's family gathers around the kitchen table. My earliest memories are centered on that yellow-painted kitchen table where I learned to become part of the rest of the world through family dynamics. While each of us—Mom, Dad, and us kids—talked about the day's events, we were indirectly examining our feelings and learning how to interact and negotiate. Today, the kitchen table is still the center of my own home. It's where I connect with my daughters, Wynonna and Ashley, my grandchildren, Elijah and Grace, Wy's husband, Arch, and my husband, Larry. It serves as our United Nations, where we get down to the nitty-gritty. And good food is always there, to nourish us and comfort us.

Although I share my personal experiences of family life, and my strategies for a positive life-style and wellness, with literally millions of people, my preference has always been the one-on-one conversation. Even when I'm onstage in an arena,

Today, the average American eats one-third of his or her meals away from home.

*Self-fulfilling prophecy:
Wy (age three) and me*

I try to connect with each person as if it's just the two of us sitting at my own kitchen table.

The Most Important Job in the World

Ask any child psychologist if they don't agree: I feel strongly that a mom should stay at home with her child for the first few years. I had to go to work when Wy was eight and Ashley only four. With today's technology, women can work at home.

When I was growing up, there were few role models for career-minded young girls. That's why I feel so strongly now about mentoring and am grateful for my real-life girlfriends who are inspiring examples of how today's women can also be trailblazers. Susan Butcher of Bush, Alaska, is the first woman to win the Iditarod, the famous dogsled race across Alaska. Susan lost two of her beloved sled dogs when a crazed moose attacked her in seventy-mile-an-hour winds; she had to kill the moose with her axe. Explorer and scientist Kathryn Sullivan, Ph.D., is very down-to-earth, yet she was the first woman to walk in space. Dr. Sylvia Earle, an oceanographer, went in the other direction, and holds the world record for the greatest depth reached as a solo untethered diver. She also studies dolphins and builds submarines with her daughter. They're all truly modern-day pioneer women.

Seventy-six percent of married women with school-age children work outside the home.
In 1950, only twenty-eight percent worked outside the home.

Dinner Conversation Appetizer: Ask each other, "What would you be doing if you knew you couldn't fail?" In other words, what is your secret fantasy?

Mom in her kitchen teaching Ashley how to make fried chicken

"*Let the mealtimes be far more than the fulfillment of a necessity. In this home, food shall be prepared with grace, and eaten with gratitude.*"

—FROM *A HOUSE BLESSING,* BY WELLERAN POLTARNESS

Polly's Fried Chicken with Tan Gravy

Practically every Sunday when I was a kid, this was the after-church dinner— Mom's delicious fried chicken with mashed potatoes and gravy. Mom believes we're spiritual beings in an earthly body. Our souls were fed in Sunday school and church, and then she fed our bodies.

My Mom Polly has always been around food. As a teenager, she was the cashier at the family-run Hamburger Inn in Ashland, the most popular gathering place in our town. Each booth and table usually had its own little powwow going on. It was there Mom learned how to cut up a whole chicken by watching her grandmother, Cora Lee Burton. Saturday night Grandma would do the chickens, soaking them overnight in salt water to keep them moist. In this recipe, my mother uses her special toasted flour to make the gravy. If you've bought already-packaged chicken parts, figure two pieces per person, more if you love leftovers. Hot or cold, this dish is always good.

MAKES 4 SERVINGS

1 whole chicken (about 3½ pounds), giblets and liver removed for other uses, cut into 8 serving pieces
Cold salted water (about 1 tablespoon of salt)
1 cup all-purpose flour
1½ teaspoons black pepper
1½ teaspoons salt
Vegetable oil, for frying (enough to come up halfway on chicken pieces—about 1½ inch depth in skillet)
Tan Gravy (recipe, page 8)

1. In a large bowl, soak the chicken in enough salted water to cover in the refrigerator overnight.

2. Drain the chicken and shake off the excess water.

3. In a pie plate, mix together the flour, pepper, and salt. (Mom lists the pepper before the salt because people often slack off on the pepper—don't!) Roll the chicken in the flour to coat.

4. Into two 12-inch cast-iron skillets, pour enough vegetable oil to come to a depth of 1½ inches in each skillet or about halfway up on the chicken pieces. Heat over medium-high heat

until very hot (350° on a deep-fat frying thermometer)—the chicken should sizzle when it hits the oil. Using tongs, carefully add the chicken pieces to the hot oil, making sure there is a lot of space between the pieces. (Fry all the chicken at the same time, but be careful not to crowd the skillets—you don't want to lower the temperature of the cooking oil.)

5. Cover the skillets and lower the heat to medium. Learn to listen to the chicken; if you don't hear it sizzling or cooking, carefully uncover the skillets to see if the oil is bubbling. If not bubbling, turn up the heat and cover the skillet immediately. After 15 minutes, the bottom sides should be brown. Turn the pieces over with the tongs, and continue to cook, covered, browning on all sides, and adjusting the heat as necessary. Remove the breast pieces after another 12 minutes—the white meat cooks faster than the dark meat. All the chicken should be cooked in about 30 minutes.

6. Transfer the chicken to paper towels to drain. Serve immediately.

Tan Gravy

MAKES 1¼ CUPS, ENOUGH
TO SERVE 3 OR 4 PEOPLE

**2 tablespoons cooking oil from the
fried chicken (page 6)**
**3 tablespoons Polly's Toasted Flour
(see page 19)**
About 1 cup milk
¼ teaspoon black pepper

1. Carefully pour the hot cooking oil
   from the chicken-frying skillets into a
   heatproof container to reuse for future
   frying. Return 2 tablespoons of the oil
   to one of the skillets and heat over
   medium-high heat.

2. Add the 3 tablespoons flour and cook,
   whisking up the browned frying bits
   from the bottom of the skillet. Let the
   mixture cook, whisking constantly,
   until a deep brown, about 3 minutes.

3. Gradually add the milk, whisking constantly, until the mixture is well
   blended and smooth. Reduce the heat
   and simmer until thickened, 3 to 5
   minutes. Add the pepper. Serve in a
   sauceboat with the fried chicken.

*The food chain: My great grandmother Cora Lee Burton with her son Carl
in her general store at the turn of the century*

*If you could have been present at any event in your family's history,
which would it have been?*

Let's All Play Family Feud: Powwow Rules

It's important to have a pleasant atmosphere when digesting food, so we have our meetings to deal with problems, separately from our meals. It's taken many years of hurt feelings, tantrums, and unresolved conflicts to get to where we are now! The room for improvement will always be the biggest room at our house.

These are the guidelines we've all agreed on:

1. No interrupting.

2. No shouting.

3. Everyone must realize we each have our own realities.

4. Everyone gets as much time as they need to express themselves completely.

5. Everyone should be prepared with their thoughts and solutions so time isn't wasted.

6. Stop and think before you speak so you talk to the person as if they were a friend instead of a relative.

7. Everyone needs to remember that these are just issues! Our commitment to communicating is the bottom line to making sure the family endures.

Chew on this a while: Conflict can't survive without your participation. Confrontation gets easier when you give up your need to be right, and no matter how you slice it, there's always two sides.

A family is like a tossed salad— each ingredient is distinct and identifiable.

Keeping two high-spirited teenagers, Wy and Ashley, in line in the kitchen on Del Rio Pike

FOOD FOR OUR FAMILY

The easiest way to get people to show up for the dinner table is to make sure the food is great! Having dinner at the same time every day helps everyone plan their schedule and make a commitment to being there. It's also important that every person looks forward to mealtime as a time to relax and be fully themselves, surrounded by people who really care about what they did during the day.

The kitchen table is a natural place to learn. My Mom would often take a file card from her recipe box and write a new word on it—like "serendipity"! My brothers and sister and I would look it up in the dictionary and then make up a sentence with it. She told us, "Reading is to the mind what exercise is to the body."

Here's one for you:
If at birth you could select
the sex and profession
your child would eventually
pursue, would you do so?

Glen Judd's Ashland Oil service station

Daddy also encouraged our love of learning. Glen Judd owned a gas station and for many years was Ashland Oil's Filling Station Operator of the Year. He'd work extra hours so I could have piano lessons and be able to take vacations to see new places. He'd give us a dime for each "A" we earned on our report cards.

When Daddy couldn't get away from work, Mom would pack up dinner in a brown paper sack, and we'd all jump into the family station wagon and drive over to the station. In a sense we were taking our kitchen table to him.

Even as a teenager, I never once ate in my bedroom. We always sat down together for our meals, with no other distractions such as television or running to answer the phone. It's these ordinary, everyday moments that shape and form our lives.

TV Has an Educational Channel— It's Called "Off"

When I met John Hendricks, founder and chairman of the Discovery Channel, I told him although I love his channel, I was also concerned that the closest some kids get to nature these days is watching the Discovery Channel. Fifty-four percent of American kids have a television in their own bedroom, and they watch it about 28 hours a week—that's losing one day a week! That adds up to watching about 16,000 murders before the age of 18. And this doesn't even include time spent on computers and video games. My advice? Get kids out of the house and outdoors!

Food for Thought: If you had a crystal ball and could ask only one question about the future, what would it be? About the past?

I've always given people affectionate nicknames. I laughed out loud when it dawned on me they're all food-related. Wy is Sweet Tater, her daughter Grace is Tater Tot, her son Elijah is Jellybean, Ashley's My Sweet Pea, Larry is Mr. Beans (don't ask), my sis Margaret's Popcorn, my niece Erin is Pumpkin, brother Mark is Nutty Buddy, my nephew Brian is Sweetie Pie, and Mom's Cheeto.

Stuff Yourself with Stuffed Pepper Cups

You're getting a whole meal in a pepper cup—vegetables, rice, and meat. As a rule, I don't like the taste of fresh green bell pepper—it's too strong. But when I steam them as I do here, the flavor becomes much milder. Like our emotions, we need to let off steam from time to time to keep them from overpowering us. Hardening of the attitudes: Did you know doctors say anger is more of a health threat than being overweight, smoking, drinking, etc.?

MAKES 6 SERVINGS

6 medium green bell peppers (or other colors)
1 pound ground beef round
1 large onion, diced
1 tablespoon Worcestershire sauce
1 can (14½ ounces) stewed tomatoes
½ cup tomato paste
2 cups cooked white or brown rice
1 can (11 ounces) corn kernels, drained
1 tablespoon dried Italian seasoning
½ teaspoon salt
1½ cups (6 ounces) shredded Cheddar cheese

1. Preheat the oven to 375°.

2. In the bottom of a large pot with a steamer basket or metal colander inside, bring 1 inch of water to a boil.

3. Slice the tops off the green peppers. Cut away the ribs and remove the seeds. Place the peppers upside down in the steamer basket. Steam, covered, until the peppers soften slightly, about 4 minutes.

4. Meanwhile, in a large, heavy skillet, brown together the meat and onion over medium-high heat, about 4 minutes. Carefully drain off excess fat. Add the Worcestershire, stewed tomatoes, and tomato paste, stirring to blend. Reduce the heat to low. Stir in the rice, corn, Italian seasoning, and salt. Heat through, stirring occasionally. Let cool slightly. Stir in ¾ cup of the shredded cheese.

5. Place the peppers upright in a casserole just large enough to hold them snugly. Fill the peppers with the meat mixture. Spoon any extra meat mixture into the casserole around the peppers. Cover loosely with aluminum foil.

6. Bake in the 375° oven for 30 minutes. Remove the foil. Sprinkle the tops of the peppers with the remaining shredded cheese. Bake, uncovered, another 10 minutes. Serve hot.

My brother Mark likes to wear his sombrero when I cook this dish for him.

Meals on Wheels

About seventy-five percent of all women don't know "what's for dinner" that evening as late as four o'clock that same afternoon. This is my trick for getting around the four o'clock rush: When I'm preparing certain dishes, I cook extra to freeze. I label them with the date and use them within four to six months, depending on what each dish is. I also cook extra

to send to folks who are ill, to Wy's house when she's recording late in the studio, and to Ashley's because she's single and doesn't always make an effort to prepare hot meals. And we have a widowed farmer neighbor, Harding Meachum, who loves it when I set food on his back porch.

When you live in the country, you depend on your neighbors.

Chili Pie

This works when you're in the mood for something Southwestern. What I particularly like about this dish is that it's made from things I usually have in the kitchen already. And once I make up my mind this is going to be dinner, it's ready for the table in less than an hour.

MAKES 6 SERVINGS

1 pound ground beef round
1 small onion, chopped
1 clove garlic, chopped, or 1 teaspoon garlic powder
1 tablespoon all-purpose flour
1 package (1⅛ ounces) chili seasoning
1 teaspoon chili powder
1 can (6 ounces) tomato paste
   + 1 can water
1 can (11 ounces) mexi-corn, drained
½ cup chopped canned black olives (optional)
1 large tube (12 ounces) Hungry Jack biscuits, extra flaky (10 biscuits)★
1 package (8 ounces) shredded Cheddar cheese (2 cups)

1. Preheat the oven to 350°.

2. Heat a large skillet over medium-high heat. Crumble in the beef. Add the onion and garlic and cook, stirring, over medium-high heat until the beef is browned and no longer pink, about

7 minutes. Drain off the excess fat. Stir in the flour and cook 1 minute, stirring. Stir in the chili seasoning, chili powder, tomato paste, water, mexicorn, and olives, if using. Bring to a boil. Then reduce the heat to low and simmer, covered, stirring twice, for about 15 minutes.

3. Meanwhile, separate the 10 biscuits from the tube, and then pull each biscuit apart in half. Place half the biscuits in the bottom of a 9-inch deep-dish pie plate. Spoon the chili mixture over the biscuits. Top with the remaining biscuits, torn side down. Sprinkle with the shredded cheese.

4. Bake in the 350° oven, uncovered, until the biscuits are browned and the cheese is melted, 16 to 18 minutes. Let stand for 10 minutes and serve while wearing a sombrero.

★ TIP

Instead of the store-bought biscuits, I like to make my own corn crust with masa harina or corn flour, which you can find in the supermarket next to the oatmeal and cornmeal. In a bowl, mix 1 cup masa harina with ½ teaspoon salt, 1 tablespoon oil, and 1 cup water. Then spread over top of chili mixture.

A wise old owl

sat in an oak.

The more he saw,

the less he spoke.

The less he spoke,

the more he heard.

Why can't we

be like that wise old bird?

We Have One Tongue and *Two* Ears!

One of the most fascinating dinner conversations we've ever had involved the work of an acquaintance named Francis Collins, M.D. and Ph.D., who's the Director for the National Center for Human Genome Research. Francis is an ethical man who says we're spiritual creatures and not "marionettes." Do you know how your family members feel about important social issues? How about turning off the TV some night and finding out. You might be surprised!

What's your guess: Who do you think normally talks the most during dinner? It's nearly a three-way tie, with twenty-nine percent answering that everyone takes turns, twenty-eight percent saying that kids talk the most, and twenty-seven percent pointing to mom as the biggest talker. Only fifteen percent point to dad. The important thing is that we not only talk to each other, but that we *listen*.

That Warm and Fuzzy Feeling

Back in 1979 the girls and I moved to the countryside outside of Nashville and were living in a 120-year-old white frame house with a gingerbread-trimmed front porch. Times were tough, but we made it warm and cozy. I had doilies on the furniture, lots of plants, and lace curtains. Everybody just flipped out when they walked into the house. The usual response would be, "This reminds me of my grandmother's house."

Cheerleader Ashley with Larry on Del Rio Pike

Magic words guaranteed to give you the last say:

Forgivee: "I'm sorry. Will you forgive me?"

Forgiver: "Yes. I'll bury the hatchet and forget where I buried it."

I had just started dating a bass singer named Larry Strickland, who had been part of the backup group for Elvis. After Elvis's death, Larry kept singing and touring with a country group. The first time he came to meet Wy and Ashley, I so wanted to make a good impression. We scrubbed the house from top to bottom, and when Larry pulled up our gravel driveway, I was waiting on the back porch in my best apron. Wy had put her great-great-grandmother Cora Lee's lace tablecloth on our old-fashioned dining room table. Ashley had picked wildflowers and put them in a mason jar. Since my nurse's paycheck didn't go very far in running our small household, I could only afford a small amount of meat for the beef stew. As I dished out dinner, I purposely spooned most of the meat into Larry's bowl. Right after we blessed the meal, twelve-year-old Ashley did something that totally busted me. She held out her spoon filled with pieces of potato and offered, "Hey Larry, trade you my potatoes for a piece of your meat." So much for first impressions! Larry caught on right away, turned red, and quietly switched bowls with Ashley.

Recently, seventeen years later, Ashley brought up this incident one evening at suppertime. We'd had no idea how it had hurt her. She felt like I was literally and figuratively taking food out of her mouth and giving it to a stranger. It reinforced my belief that food is more than nutrition—it conveys love. We must never forget that children are always hungry for our attention and affection.

By Gosh! Beef Stew

This is the very first meal I served to Mr. Cool, my future husband. Our courtship has now lasted eighteen years. Larry and I have discovered marriage multiplies joy and divides sorrow. Remember, the mate you choose will determine about ninety percent of either your happiness or misery. I disagree with the misleading statement that marriage should be fifty/fifty; two halves don't make a whole when we look for someone else to make us happy. I believe each partner has to be fully one hundred percent. It's not so much just finding the right person as it is *being* the right person. As Marilyn Monroe said, "It's better to be unhappy alone than unhappy with someone!"

MAKES 8 SERVINGS

- ⅓ cup all-purpose flour
- 1 teaspoon paprika
- ½ teaspoon salt
- ¼ teaspoon pepper
- 2 pounds round steak, trimmed of excess fat, and cut into 1-inch squares
- 3 tablespoons olive oil
- 1 tablespoon Worcestershire sauce
- 4½ cups beef broth
- 1 bay leaf
- 2 medium onions, chopped
- 4 carrots, trimmed, sliced
- 2 stalks celery, with leaves, halved lengthwise and thickly sliced
- 4 cups 1-inch cubes peeled Idaho baking potatoes
- ¼ cup Polly's Toasted Flour (see page 19)
- ½ envelope brown gravy mix
- 2 teaspoons fresh lemon juice
- 1 teaspoon dried thyme
- ½ teaspoon salt
- ¼ teaspoon black pepper

1. In a plastic food-storage bag, combine the flour, paprika, salt, and pepper. Add half of the meat and shake to coat. Remove the meat, shaking off the excess flour. Repeat with the remaining half of the meat.

2. In a large, heavy Dutch oven, heat half of the oil. Add half of the meat and brown on all sides, about 8 minutes. Add half of the Worcestershire sauce and then remove the meat to a plate. Repeat with the remaining oil, meat, and Worcestershire. Return all the meat to the pot and add enough beef broth to the pot to barely cover the meat, about 2 cups. Add the bay leaf. Simmer, covered, for 1 hour.

Larry was Elvis's bass singer. After the king's death, Larry formed a country group called Memphis.

3. Add the onion, carrot, celery, and potato to the pot.

4. In a small bowl, stir together the remaining beef broth, the Toasted Flour, the brown gravy mix and the lemon juice. Stir the mixture into the pot along with the thyme, salt, and pepper. There should be enough liquid to cover the vegetables; if not, add more broth as needed. Simmer, covered, over low heat, stirring occasionally, until the beef and vegetables are fork-tender, about 45 minutes. Taste, and add seasonings if necessary. Fish out the bay leaf, if you can, and discard. Serve without guilt.

POLLY'S TOASTED FLOUR

In a dry 9-inch cast-iron skillet, spread all-purpose flour to a depth of ¼ inch, about 1 cup. Place the skillet over low to medium heat and cook the flour, stirring, and watching closely, until it turns a light brown color, 12 to 15 minutes. Remove to a bowl, let cool, and store in a tightly covered container in a cool, dry place. This will keep for months.

Crunchy Chicken Casserole

My family loves casseroles. This is an easy one—everything gets mixed in one bowl and then spooned into the casserole.

MAKES 6 SERVINGS

- 3 packed cups shredded cooked chicken breast (about 1 pound)
- 1 cup mayonnaise
- ¾ cup sliced celery
- 2 cans (8 ounces each) sliced water chestnuts, drained and rinsed
- ½ cup sour cream
- ⅓ cup bread crumbs, either fresh or plain dried

1. Preheat the oven to 350° degrees.

2. In a large bowl, mix together the chicken, mayonnaise, celery, water chestnuts, and sour cream. Scrape into an 11 × 7 × 2-inch or other 2-quart baking dish. Sprinkle the top with the bread crumbs.

3. Bake in the 350° oven until the edges are browned, the casserole is bubbly, and the crumbs are lightly golden, 20 to 25 minutes. Let the casserole stand for 10 minutes before serving.

Homemade Arts and Crafts

When I was putting myself through college and nursing school and the girls were little, I used to buy the frozen chicken pot pies in the aluminum containers. Wy would wash the containers out after dinner and save them for her paints. She was a very expressive child who loved to draw and paint. Together we would create our own greeting cards and paint pictures for the grandparents to put on their refrigerator doors. Equally imaginative, Ashley shaped small pieces of clay into fanciful designs and then baked them on a cookie sheet. After they hardened and cooled, Ashley glued tiny safety pins on the backs to create brooches and other kinds of jewelry. As the kids got older, we made candles, soap, and Christmas ornaments to give as homemade gifts.

Preparing meals and cleaning up afterward is also a wonderful opportunity to let the kids help out and spend time one-on-one together.

Why did the chicken cross the road? To prove to the possum it could be done!

What do you call a chicken crossing the road? Poultry in motion.

Cutting homemade soap for our personal use and to give as gifts

Chicken Pot Pie

From scratch is always best. Starting out with a whole chicken is what makes this good—no shortcuts here. Sometimes to make something good, you have to work at it. This could be your masterpiece.

MAKES 10 TO 12 SERVINGS

CRUST

3 cups all-purpose flour

1 teaspoon salt

1 cup solid vegetable shortening

1 large egg

1 tablespoon distilled white vinegar

4 to 5 tablespoons ice water

CHICKEN FILLING

1 whole chicken (about 3½ pounds), giblets and liver removed for other uses

5 medium all-purpose potatoes, peeled and cut into ¾-inch chunks

3 medium carrots, trimmed and sliced ¼ inch thick

2 stalks celery, trimmed and sliced ¼ inch thick

1 medium onion, diced

1 can (10¾ ounces) condensed cream of chicken soup, undiluted

1 container (16 ounces) sour cream

1 can (8½ ounces) tiny green peas, drained

½ teaspoon salt

½ teaspoon black pepper

1. *Make the crust:* In a large bowl, stir together the flour and salt. Using a pastry blender or 2 knives used like a scissors, cut in the shortening until the mixture resembles coarse crumbs. In a small bowl, mix together the egg, vinegar, and 4 tablespoons of the ice water. Drizzle over the flour mixture, tossing with a fork, until the dough comes together (if the dough seems a little dry, add the remaining tablespoon water). With your hands, press the dough into a ball. Divide into 2 pieces, one slightly larger than the other. Flatten into 2 disks, 1 inch thick. Wrap each in plastic wrap and refrigerate for at least 30 minutes.

2. *Meanwhile, make the filling:* In a 6-quart pot, place the chicken. Cover with cold water and bring to a boil. Lower the heat and simmer until the thigh meat of the chicken is no longer pink near the bone, about 45 minutes. Remove the chicken from the pot. Reserve the cooking liquid.

3. Bring the cooking liquid to a boil over medium-high heat. Add the potato, carrot, celery, and onion. Return to the boil and cook until the potato chunks are just tender and still hold their shape, about 10 minutes. Drain, reserving the cooking liquid for soup-making or for other uses.

4. When the chicken is cool enough to handle, remove the skin and bones and discard. Cut the chicken meat into bite-size pieces.

5. In a large bowl, stir together the soup and sour cream. Fold in the chicken and the vegetables, including the peas. Stir in the salt and pepper.

6. Preheat the oven to 350°.

7. *Roll out the dough:* On a lightly floured surface, with a lightly floured rolling pin, roll out the larger disk of dough into a 13-inch circle. Ease the circle into a 9-inch deep-dish pie plate. Gently press the dough against the sides and bottom of the plate. Trim the edges to a ¾-inch overhang. Roll out the remaining dough into a 12-inch circle and drape it over the rolling pin.

8. *To assemble the pie:* Spoon the chicken filling into the crust-lined pie plate, mounding it in the center. Unroll the dough from the rolling pin over the filling. Seal the edges together and flute. Cut several steam vents in the top of the pie.

9. Place a sheet of aluminum foil on the bottom rack in the oven to catch any drips. Bake the pie in the 350° oven until the crust is lightly golden and the filling is bubbly, about 1 hour and 45 minutes. Transfer the pie to a wire rack and let stand for 20 minutes before serving.

TIP

You can cut out little chickens, stars, or other shapes from the dough with cookie cutters and place them on top of the crust.

Why does a chicken coop have only two doors? 'Cause if it had four doors it would be a chicken sedan.

Get Your Wordsworth

Ashley and I share a love of language. If words are the clothes our thoughts wear, then Ashley is very well dressed! Once Wynonna asked her, "What's an oxymoron?" Ashley explained, "It's when you put two words together that really contradict each other, such as jumbo shrimp, military intelligence, friendly fire, and uncontested divorce." All children learn more by example than by what you say. I've learned the hard way that what you do shouts a heck of a lot louder and drowns out your words.

I suggest you spend more time and less money on your kids.

Ashley and Wy didn't realize we were poor, because they felt loved and safe.

Shrimp Kabobs— Grill of My Dreams

I had never tasted asparagus or shrimp until I was 16 and on a date. Serve these kabobs on a bed of rice, white or otherwise. And you can grill asparagus or wrap buttered ears of corn in foil and cook them while the coals are hot. If you don't already have one—get a grip and get a grill! More and more people are developing a fear of frying.

MAKES 4 SERVINGS

2 dozen large shrimp (25 to 30 per pound), shelled and deveined
16 cherry tomatoes
16 large fresh mushrooms
1 medium yellow bell pepper, stemmed, seeded, and cut into 16 square pieces
1 small can (8 ounces) pineapple chunks, packed in juice, drained

BASTING MIXTURE
½ cup olive oil
1 teaspoon garlic salt
½ teaspoon dried basil
½ teaspoon black pepper

1. Prepare a grill with medium-hot coals, or preheat the broiler.

2. On each of 8 metal skewers, alternately thread 3 shrimp and 2 pieces of any of the vegetables and fruit.

3. *Make the basting mixture:* In a small bowl, stir together the oil, garlic salt, basil, and pepper. Brush the kabobs with the basting mixture.

4. Grill or broil the kabobs 4 to 6 inches from the heat, basting occasionally and turning, until shrimp are pink and vegetables are lightly browned and tender, 8 to 10 minutes. Serve immediately.

What's the difference between the Judds and the Girl Scouts? The Girl Scouts have adult supervision!

Eight-year-old Wynonna and fellow Brownie Astrid Santic

Best Brownies, Ever!

A brownie is one of those foods that people have very definite opinions about. Their version is the best, and everything else is a distant second. So, in the spirit of compromise and negotiation, this recipe attempts to appease two very different tastes in brownies. It's based on a recipe from the *Joy of Cooking,* that American classic. If you like brownies fudgy and moist, bake them in a 13 × 9 × 2-inch pan. For a more cakelike version, use a 9 × 9 × 2-inch square. And yes, I was a Brownie leader.

MAKES 9 LARGE BROWNIES,
OR WHATEVER SIZE YOU LIKE

1 stick or ½ cup butter

4 ounces unsweetened chocolate, chopped

4 large eggs

¼ teaspoon salt

2 cups sugar

1 teaspoon pure vanilla extract

1 cup all-purpose flour

1 cup chopped pecans

1. In a small saucepan, melt together the butter and chocolate, stirring occasionally. It's very important to let the mixture cool before using.

2. Preheat the oven to 350°. Butter a 13 × 9 × 2-inch baking pan or 9 × 9 × 2-inch square baking pan.

3. In a medium bowl, with an electric mixer at medium speed, beat together the eggs and salt until light and foamy, about 3 minutes. Beat in the butter mixture until blended. Then beat in the sugar and vanilla until well mixed. With a rubber spatula, fold in the flour and pecans. Scrape into the prepared pan.

4. Bake the 13 × 9 × 2-inch pan in the 350° oven until still slightly soft to the touch and a wooden pick inserted in the center comes out with crumbs attached to it, about 30 minutes. Or bake the 9 × 9 × 2-inch square pan for 40 minutes. Transfer the pan to a wire rack to cool. Cover and refrigerate until chilled. Then cut into rectangles or squares, as large or as small as you want.

Hand over that chocolate and no one will get hurt! Chocolate fact: You'd have to eat a half pound of chocolate to get the amount of caffeine in one cup of coffee.

More Food for Thought: If you could change one thing about your family, what would it be? What is your favorite trait in each member? What dominant personality traits seem to be passed from one generation to another?

Simplest Chocolate Mousse

If you're craving something sweet, this takes no time at all, except for the chilling.

MAKES 4 SERVINGS

> **4 ounces German sweet chocolate, chopped**
> **3 tablespoons water**
> **1 teaspoon pure vanilla extract**
> **2 cups frozen nondairy whipped topping, thawed**

1. In a small, heavy saucepan, melt the chocolate with the water over low heat. Let cool.

2. Stir in the vanilla. Transfer to a medium bowl. With a rubber spatula, fold in the whipped topping. Cover and refrigerate until well chilled, about 2 hours.

The Judd women at a family reunion: (left to right, back row) Wy, Grace, Ashley, niece Erin, and sister-in-law Middy; (front row) Mom, me with Boogaloo, and Margaret

IT CAN ONLY GET BETTER: COMFORT FOOD

Food fulfills all sorts of needs physically as well as psychologically. People with weight problems often eat to feed an emotional or spiritual void. It can be an addiction. Certain foods provide comfort because they take us back to an easier, safer time. Everyone in my family has his or her own special comfort food.

We now have documented evidence that a strong social network greatly aids health. A large-scale seventeen-year study of health factors—including obesity, alcohol, and smoking—revealed that having close ties with other people outweighs in a positive manner all other influences on health and longevity.

The average person spends two hours a day feeling guilty about the unimportant things in life.

Guilt and worry are both vampires that suck the life force out of us.

Wynonna's Cherry Jell-O Salad

Growing up, my daughter Wynonna loved Jell-O salad—she still does. It's her comfort food. One day I didn't have her Jell-O salad on the second shelf in the refrigerator, on the left-hand side, and she hollered at me, "Mommy, you don't love me anymore!" Isn't it funny how we show love for each other and how we're comforted by little things. No need to go out and buy fancy, expensive gifts. Little, everyday things are often enough—more than enough.

This is even better served the day after it's made. For a special treat, serve with a little dab of Curry Mayonnaise (page 203) on top.

MAKES 6 SERVINGS★

2 cups water

1 box (6 ounces) cherry-flavored Jell-O

1 small can (about 8 ounces) fruit cocktail, drained

1 banana, diced

½ cup chopped walnuts

1. In a medium saucepan, bring the 2 cups of water to a boil. Stir in the Jell-O until dissolved. Remove from the heat. Stir in the fruit cocktail, banana, and nuts.

2. Pour into an 8 × 8 × 2-inch square baking pan, a 4-cup mold or bowl, or seven ½-cup individual molds. Refrigerate until firm, about 4 hours. Unmold, if you like.

TIP

If you make this salad as in the recipe, the solids will rise to the top, leaving a band of clear Jell-O. If you unmold the salad, this clear band will be on the top. To evenly distribute the fruit and nuts through the salad, first chill the Jell-O, without any additions, until it has the consistency of raw egg whites. Then fold in the fruits and nuts.

★If you use the 7 individual molds, there's one extra for the cook.

Try asking your family what their attachments are to foods and what particular food memories they have.

Wy celebrated her birthday every May while we were recording in the studio with our producers Brent and Don. I always made enough cake for all the musicians.

Tuna Noodle Casserole

When I was a single mom, this was a staple. I still make it for Wynonna and Ashley when their mood rings are an ugly shade.

MAKES 4 TO 6 SERVINGS

- **2 cans (6 ounces each) solid white tuna packed in oil, drained well and flaked**
- **2 cans (10¾ ounces each) condensed cream of mushroom soup or cream of chicken soup, undiluted, or 1 can of each**
- **1½ cups cooked egg noodles (about 2 cups, uncooked)**
- **⅛ teaspoon black pepper**
- **½ cup crushed cracker crumbs (optional—we prefer without)**

1. Preheat the oven to 350°.

2. In a medium bowl, mix together the tuna, soup, cooked noodles, and pepper. Spoon into a 9 × 5 × 3-inch loaf pan. Sprinkle the top with the cracker crumbs, if using.

3. Bake, uncovered, in the 350° oven until the filling is bubbly and the crumbs are toasted, 30 to 35 minutes. Let stand for 10 minutes before serving.

Home is where they <u>have</u> to take you in—it's where they know all your faults but still accept you anyway.

Myrtie's Mighty Fine Chicken and Dumplins

When you marry, it makes life so much easier and more enjoyable if you love your mate's family. I love my hubby's family and am grateful to him for not comparing my cooking to his mom's, 'cause she's a good cook! I heard that Princess Diana really left Prince Charles because he was forever comparing her (chef's) cooking with his mom's (chef's) cooking.

MAKES 6 TO 8 SERVINGS

- **1 large chicken fryer (about 3½ pounds), washed and cut into pieces**
- **2 stalks celery, cut up**
- **6 cups chicken broth, in can or fresh**
- **2½ cups all-purpose flour**
- **½ teaspoon salt**
- **1 cup water, as needed**
- **Salt, to taste**
- **Pepper, to taste**
- **¼ cup heavy cream or milk**

1. In a large pot, place the chicken and add the celery and the 6 cups broth. Bring to a boil and then gently boil, covered, until the chicken is tender and no longer pink near the bone, about 45 minutes. Remove the chicken from the broth and let cool. When cool enough to handle, remove the skin and bones and discard. Pull the meat into bite-size pieces. Set aside. Remove the celery and discard. Keep the broth boiling, uncovered, over medium heat.

2. Meanwhile, in a large bowl, mix together the flour and the ½ teaspoon salt. Add the water a little at a time, tossing with a fork, until the dough is a good consistency for rolling out. Divide the dough into fourths.

3. Roll out one fourth of the dough as thin as possible, the thinner the better. Cut into 2- to 2½-inch squares. Drop the squares one at a time into the boiling broth. Repeat with the remaining dough. Watch the pot to make sure it doesn't boil over. If the broth gets too thick, add a little hot water, not cold. As you add the dough squares, do not stir, because the dough will stick together in a ball. Instead, flip them around with a fork to keep them separate. Season with salt and pepper to taste.

4. Turn the heat to low. Stir in the chicken pieces and the cream or milk. Simmer for 10 minutes, and then serve.

Broth is like a Southern debutante—it should be from good stock.

Myrtie and Rev. Ralph Strickland celebrating their 50th wedding anniversary in 1991

Reverend Ralph's Chocolate Pudding

Ashley claims she can eat her weight in this. Ever since she was little, one of Ashley's food rewards was chocolate pudding. When Ms. Phi Beta Kappa came home for a weekend from the University of Kentucky, and I'd be on tour with Wynonna, I would arrange to have someone else make the pudding and put it on the second shelf in the refrigerator for her. My girls are as eccentric as their Mom. The pudding recipe here comes from my father-in-law, the Reverend Ralph Strickland of North Carolina, whom I adore.

Homework: Have each school-age child and the adults in the family learn the beliefs of a major world religion to discuss at the table. The highest form of ignorance is to reject something we know nothing about.

Ashley celebrating completion of filming her movie Heat, with another leading man, "Grandpa Ralph"

MAKES 8 SERVINGS

- 2 cups sugar
- ¼ cup unsweetened cocoa powder
- ¼ cup all-purpose flour
- 1 teaspoon cornstarch
- Pinch of salt
- 4 large eggs
- 2 cups milk
- 2 tablespoons butter or margarine
- 2 teaspoons pure vanilla extract

1. In a medium saucepan, whisk together the sugar, cocoa powder, flour, cornstarch, and salt until blended. Whisk in the eggs and milk until smooth.

2. Cook over medium heat, stirring constantly, until thickened and boiling, 6 to 8 minutes. Cook another 2 minutes. Remove the saucepan from the heat. Stir in the butter and vanilla. Place a piece of waxed paper directly on the surface of the pudding. Let cool. Serve with a spoonful of whipped cream and a Sugar Cookie (page 154), for added fun.

There's no evidence that chocolate causes acne. It's not chocolate that promotes tooth decay—it's the sugar. So, what are you waiting for?

Ashley's Four-Layered Dessert

This is another of Ashley's favorites. It uses a thicker version of the chocolate pudding on page 34. Warning: It's a girdle buster!

MAKES 8 SERVINGS

FIRST LAYER

1 stick or ½ cup butter

1 cup all-purpose flour

¾ cup chopped pecans

THIRD LAYER

1 cup sugar

⅓ cup unsweetened cocoa powder

3 tablespoons all-purpose flour

2 tablespoons cornstarch

Pinch of salt

3 large egg yolks

2 cups milk

2 tablespoons butter or margarine

2 teaspoons pure vanilla extract

SECOND LAYER

½ cup heavy cream, or 1 cup nondairy whipped topping

1 package (8 ounces) cream cheese, at room temperature

1 cup confectioners' sugar

FOURTH LAYER

1 cup heavy cream, or 2 cups
nondairy whipped topping

⅓ cup chopped pecans

1. Preheat the oven to 350°. Line an 8 × 8 × 2-inch square pan with aluminum foil. Coat lightly with nonstick cooking spray.

2. *Make the first layer:* In a small saucepan, melt the butter. Stir in the flour until well blended. Stir in the pecans. Scrape into the prepared baking pan and press evenly over the bottom of the pan.

3. Bake in the 350° oven until browned, about 20 minutes. Transfer the pan to a wire rack to cool.

4. *Meanwhile, make the chocolate layer, which will be the third layer:* In a medium saucepan, whisk together the sugar, cocoa powder, flour, cornstarch, and salt. Whisk in the egg yolks and milk until well blended and smooth. Cook, stirring, over medium heat until thickened and boiling, 6 to 8 minutes. Stir in the butter and vanilla. Scrape into a bowl. Place a piece of waxed paper directly on the surface of the mixture, and let cool, about 30 minutes.

5. *Make the second layer:* In a medium bowl, with an electric mixer on medium speed, beat the cream, if using, until stiff peaks form. In another bowl, beat together the cream cheese and confectioners' sugar until smooth. Add the whipped cream or nondairy whipped topping and, at low speed, beat just until blended. Spread over the cooled first layer in the baking pan.

6. *To form the third layer:* Spread the chocolate mixture over the cream cheese layer. Place a piece of waxed paper directly on the surface of the mixture and refrigerate for at least 3 hours or until firm and chilled through. (You can make the recipe up to this point a day ahead.)

7. *Make the fourth layer:* Remove the waxed paper from the top. In a medium bowl, with an electric mixer at medium speed, beat the heavy cream until stiff peaks form. Spread the top with the whipped cream or the nondairy whipped topping. Sprinkle with the nuts. Lift out of the pan and cut into 8 squares.

Ashley's a wild woman in the kitchen. How can one person make such a mess?

"Seize the moment. Remember all those women on the Titanic who waved off the dessert cart."

—ERMA BOMBECK

Broke: Beans, Bread, Bologna

Before we made it in country music, Wy, Ashley, and I ate a lot of bologna and crackers, beans, and cornbread. We heated our drafty old farmhouse on Del Rio Pike with a woodstove in Wynonna's room. When Larry would come in off the road from singing at nightclubs and eating at hamburger joints and truckstops, his favorite homecoming meal was stuffed pork chops, gravy, yellow rice, and peas.

When Larry and I married, he sold his tour bus and disbanded his group. Today, Larry is President of The Judd House, our office in an historic house off the town square in Franklin, Tennessee, where he manages Wy and me and oversees a staff of a dozen people.

When Larry has a difficult day, he'll call home and ask for his comfort meal. The more things change, the more they remain the same.

*My heart burns for you, Baby!
In a recent survey, thirty-four percent
of the men questioned said heartburn
interfered with their sex lives! What better
reason to serve a comfort meal?*

Stuffed Pork Chops for Larry

Sometimes I serve this with Green Beans with Bacon (page 144).

MAKES 4 SERVINGS

½ stick or ¼ cup butter

¾ cup diced onion

¾ cup diced celery

1 teaspoon ground sage

1¾ cups water

1 container (6 ounces) stove-top stuffing

4 thick, center-cut pork chops (about 2 pounds)

1. In a medium saucepan or skillet, melt the butter over medium heat. Add the onion and celery and cook, stirring occasionally, until softened, 8 to 10 minutes.

2. Stir in the sage and the 1¾ cups water. Bring to a boil and then stir in the stuffing mix. Remove the saucepan from the heat and let stand for 5 minutes. Stir the stuffing with a fork to fluff.

3. Preheat the oven to 350°. Grease a 13 × 9 × 2-inch baking dish.

4. Meanwhile, cut a slit in the side of each chop to form a pocket. Stuff each chop

with about ½ cup of the stuffing. Place the chops in the prepared baking dish and spoon the remaining stuffing around the chops. Cover the baking dish with aluminum foil.

5. Bake in the 350° oven until the chops are tender and no longer pink in the center, about 40 minutes. Remove the foil from the dish and bake another 10 minutes. Serve immediately.

Feminism: The radical notion that women are people.

Evening at home is our quiet time together.

How to Be a Good Wife

The following are some tips taken from a 1950s high-school home economics textbook. I'm not making this up, and it's not from David Letterman's Top Ten List.

- *Have dinner ready.* Plan ahead, even the night before, to have a delicious meal on time. This is a way of letting him know that *you have been thinking about him* and are concerned about his needs. Most men are hungry when they come home, and the prospect of a good meal is part of the warm welcome needed.

- *Prepare yourself.* Take fifteen minutes to rest so that *you will be refreshed* when he arrives. Touch up your makeup, put a ribbon in your hair, and be fresh-looking. He has been with a lot of work-weary people. His boring day may need a lift.

- *Clear away clutter.* Make one last trip through the main part of the house just before your husband arrives, gathering up school books, toys, papers, etc. Then run a dust cloth over the tables. Your husband will feel he has reached a haven of rest and order, and it will give you a lift, too.

- *Prepare the children.* Take a few minutes to wash the children's hands and faces (if they are small), comb their hair, and if necessary change their clothes. They are little treasures and he would like to see them playing the part.

- *Don't greet him with problems or complaints.* Don't complain if he is late for dinner. Count this as minor compared to what he might have gone through that day.

- *Make him comfortable.* Have him lean back in a comfortable chair or suggest that he lie down in the bedroom. Have a cool or warm drink ready for him. Arrange his pillow and offer to take off his shoes. Speak in a low, soft, soothing, and pleasant voice.

- *Listen to him.* You may have a dozen things to tell him, but the moment of *his arrival* is not the time. Let him talk first.

- *Make the evening his.* Never complain if he does not take you out to dinner or to other pleasant entertainment. Instead, try to understand his world of strain and pressure, his need to unwind and relax.

Sorry ladies. There was no page on "How to Be a Good Husband."

But I did find something else . . .

Grilled Chicken with Penne

This is one of my favorite chicken dishes—my comfort food. I even pamper myself while I'm preparing it by listening to audiotapes on healing and other interesting subjects. Books on tape *are* the greatest thing since sliced bread.

MAKES 6 SERVINGS

- 2 cans (13¾ ounces each) chicken broth
- ¼ cup finely chopped garlic
- 4 boneless, skinned chicken breast halves
- ½ cup olive oil
- 1 red bell pepper, julienned (cut into matchstick-size pieces)
- 1 yellow bell pepper, julienned
- 2 cups dry-pack sun-dried tomatoes, julienned
- 1 zucchini, julienned
- ½ eggplant, julienned
- ¾ teaspoon salt
- ¼ teaspoon pepper
- 3 cups uncooked penne pasta
- ¾ cup pine nuts
- Grated Parmesan cheese, as desired

1. In a large, heavy saucepan, combine the chicken broth and garlic. Bring to a boil, cover, and then set aside for at least 15 minutes.

2. Meanwhile, grill the chicken breasts over medium-hot coals or broil until no longer pink in center, 5 to 6 minutes per side. Cut into bite-size pieces. Reserve.

3. Return saucepan with broth-and-garlic mixture to low heat. Stir in the oil. Bring to a simmer. Add the bell peppers and sun-dried tomatoes and cook, covered, 2 minutes. Add the zucchini, eggplant, salt, and pepper. Simmer until all the vegetables are tender, about 5 minutes more. Add the chicken. Remove from the heat and cover to keep warm.

4. In a large saucepan, in boiling water, cook the pasta until tender, 9 to 10 minutes. For more flavor, I add a little chicken broth to the cooking water. Drain pasta well. Add to the saucepan with the vegetables. Add the pine nuts and serve. Sprinkle with the Parmesan, as desired.

I believe the decline of the traditional family and its belief system is the most serious problem facing our country. The best each of us can do is to focus on our own home, marriage, kids, and family.

Let's get back to basics.

These are my reasons to cook:

love,

Nutrition,

tradition,

and

celebration

• **Body, Mind, and Spirit Connection**   • **On the Road**

• **Welcome Home**   • **Slow Down and Simplify: "My Cup of Solitude"**

• **Times of Sickness and Health**   • **Dinner on the Ground**

BODY, MIND, AND SPIRIT CONNECTION

Nutrition is so much more than nourishment for our physical bodies. There is nutrition for the mind and soul as well. In this chapter we'll look at ways to understand and improve our health, our emotions, and our spiritual life. I'll serve up some food for thought so tantalizing I bet you'll come back for seconds!

What you believe and how you think play a profound part in producing health problems but can also prevent and alleviate them. While I was a nurse, I saw firsthand how this worked in my patients. Later on, after being diagnosed with chronic-active hepatitis, I utilized the power of the mind in the healing process of my own body. In the last few years, I have gathered scientific data that confirms this body, mind, and spirit connection.

My good friend Dr. Andrew Weil, a Harvard graduate and one of the most prominent and credible doctors in our crusade to combine modern medicine with timeless natural wisdom, tells us that the body hears and believes everything the mind says—your body speaks your mind!

When you learn, teach. When you get, give. I guess I'm teaching what I need to continually learn as I travel around the country on the lecture circuit sharing my exciting discoveries about prevention, wellness, personal improvement, psychology, and inner peace.

Communicating with real people is what I call the "exquisite reality."

Psychoanalyst Carl Jung declared that in all aspects of our lives, spirituality is central to our growth and our ongoing healing. Self-awareness and contemplation are avenues to living truthfully. Socrates stated it a different way: "The unexamined life isn't worth living."

Our daily lives are all filled with endless responsibilities and duties. We must take care of our families, our homes, our jobs, etc. However, in order to minister to others, we must first take care of ourselves. You give out of your overflow.

When I return home after a speaking-engagement tour or public appearance, I am not just physically exhausted but emotionally drained as well. At these times, it is crucial that I practice good nutrition for my body, mind, and spirit. I've made my home my personal wilderness temple, my psychological fortress, my recess playground. I'll share with you the steps I use to slow down and simplify and enjoy. Here are some recipes for a healthy life-style.

I wish people were more tuned into and appreciative of our earth.

ON THE ROAD

Someone who heard Wy and I lived on a bus asked us, "Don't the other passengers recognize you and bug you?" When we quit laughing, we explained that it wasn't a Greyhound bus, but a Silver Eagle tour bus that was a veritable home on wheels. And we call it the Dreamchaser.

Traveling year-round in the 1980s, border to border, coast to coast, Wy and I created a mobile community with our road crew (our tribe) and by visiting with the fans (neighbors) in each state.

A typical day went something like this. Wy and I performed two shows at the San Antonio rodeo every year—a matinee and one evening performance. After the first concert, we'd hustle back onto the bus, where we'd change into our rhinestone-free flannel pajamas. I'd pull out the electric wok and stir-fry up a meal of flank steak with vegetables. And there we would all be, our tribe—road manager, bus driver, bodyguard, and Wy and me—sitting around the big kitchen booth in the front of the bus having our powwow. I asked the group: If an eccentric millionaire offered to donate a million dollars to your favorite charity, would you walk naked down a busy street? If he offered to give you the money instead, would you do it? It's from those times that I've come up with some of the "food for thought" topics I've sprinkled throughout the book.

I love to come up with road code names when we check into hotels: Patti Melt, Barb Becue, Sue Shi, Polly Esther, Ilene and Ben Dover, Barb Wire, Ann Cestors, and Mike Raphone. Can you think of any?

Meanwhile, outside, thousands of fans would be walking around the bus, trying to get a peek at the glamour queens inside. The windows were tinted, so they couldn't see the "real" us! After our meal, Wy dared me, teasing, "Okay, Mom, I don't have a million dollars, but if you get off the bus looking just the way you are, I'll rub your feet." Always willing to call someone's bluff, I jumped off the bus in my p.j.'s to a hail of flashbulbs.

Boogaloo is my companion on the Dreamchaser.

When the Dreamchaser is my traveling home, the fans become my neighbors.

Aw, Quit Your Beefin'!

The average American eats sixty-five pounds of beef a year. It's the number-one source of saturated fat in our diets. My younger daughter Ashley has been a vegetarian for many years, and now there is increasing evidence that a meatless diet offers all kinds of health benefits. We've always known fresh veggies are great for us, and the darker the color the better.

Studies done in 1997 reveal that folic acid in dark green leafy vegetables, such as spinach and broccoli, may decrease the risk of colon cancer by a third. A carrot a day has been shown by one study to cut your chance of stroke by 68 percent. And there is some evidence that fresh ginger helps reduce cholesterol levels in the blood, and can calm nausea. Did you know a diet high in veggies and fruit and low in fat can in some cases decrease blood pressure just as effectively as drugs, and without all the side effects? Combine this kind of diet with relaxation techniques and you'll see results in a matter of weeks.

Good Things Come in Weird Shapes

Did you realize that the mushroom isn't a vegetable, but an edible fungus that's good for you? It contains protein, fiber, vitamin C, and potassium. Maitake is a particular mushroom thought to increase the body's resistance to disease.

Serve up some Food for Thought. Ask at the dinner table: "What was the best year of your life? The worst? What do you want to be doing five years from now?"

Naomi's Favorite Bus Meal

A wok and a slow-cooker come in handy if you ever travel on a bus or in a camper, or live in a small apartment. This stir-fry dish is good with any of your favorite steamed fresh vegetables, such as broccoli, spinach, green beans, or zucchini. There's just 2 ounces of meat per serving in this dish, but often I omit the meat and just do the veggies and serve them over brown rice with soy sauce.

MAKES 4 SERVINGS

2 tablespoons peanut oil, or more as needed

½ pound flank steak, thinly sliced across the grain

2 medium carrots, trimmed and thinly sliced

1 cup broccoli pieces (optional)

1 cup green beans, in pieces (optional)

1 can (8 ounces) sliced water chestnuts, drained

2 cups sliced fresh mushrooms

1 medium onion, chopped

1 tablespoon minced fresh ginger

1 cup snow peas, strings removed

2 tablespoons soy sauce

4 ounces fresh spinach leaves (5 cups tightly packed), washed and tough stems removed

2 cups cooked brown rice

1. In a large wok or nonstick skillet, heat the 2 tablespoons oil over medium-high heat. Add the meat and stir-fry until no longer pink, about 1 minute. Remove the meat. Add the carrots, the broccoli and green beans, if using, the water chestnuts, mushrooms, onion, and ginger, and more oil if needed. Stir-fry until crisp-tender, about 3 minutes.

2. Return the meat to the wok and stir in the snow peas and soy sauce. Cover with the spinach leaves, then cover the wok and heat through until the spinach is wilted, 1 to 2 minutes. Serve over brown rice.

Singing for Her Supper

When my dear friend Tammy Wynette cooks her slow-cooker pork chops, she doesn't set the timer. This is her timing method: "Before a concert, I start by doing my hair and makeup. Then I get out the bus's cutting board, assemble the pork chops and other ingredients, and put it all in the slow-cooker. Next, I put on my designer dress. Then it's off the bus, walk to the stage, do the concert, get back on the bus, talk to a few radio people, sign some autographs, and take off the fancy outfit and high heels. I put on a robe and slippers and have my little dog Killer beside me. Ding—the chops are done. It's time to sit down for dinner."

We've toured with Randy Travis and Tammy Wynette—fellow artists are our extended family on the road.

Did You Ever See a Bigger Pair of ...

When Dolly Parton and I get together, we act like a couple of boobs. When I asked her what she was most proud of—her singing, songwriting, acting, or business success—she quickly replied, "Losing my weight has been my biggest accomplishment." Dolly told me she did it by eating mini meals, five to six small portions throughout the day. This can also keep your cholesterol down—if you eat the right foods—keep your blood sugar stable, and prevent heartburn from overeating.

I once asked Dolly how long it took her to do her hair. "I don't know," she answered, "I wasn't there."

Tammy Wynette's Favorite Bus Recipe

You can serve these pork chops with rice or noodles, and a tossed vegetable salad or just a plain wedge of lettuce and a tomato.

MAKES 4 SERVINGS

> 2 cans (10¾ ounces each) condensed cream of mushroom soup, undiluted
> 2 cans (7 ounces each) sliced mushrooms, drained (optional)
> 1½ teaspoons dried thyme (optional)
> ¾ teaspoon garlic powder
> ½ teaspoon black pepper
> 4 thin-sliced, center-cut pan-fry pork chops (about 1 pound)

In a slow-cooker, stir together the soup, the mushrooms and thyme, if using, the garlic powder, and pepper. Place the chops in the slow-cooker, pushing them down into the sauce. Cover and cook on high heat until tender, about 3 hours. That's all there is to it.

Never Let Others Tell You Who You Are

One night Wynonna, Ashley, and I pulled our buses and semis into a Cracker Barrel parking lot. We were just starting to become popular, and our songs were getting a lot of airplay. The restaurant was really crowded and when our food arrived, we bowed our heads like we always do, held hands, and were ready to say grace. All of a sudden I realized that everyone in the restaurant was staring at us. I wondered, should I go ahead and ask the blessing for this meal? In a split second, I realized that just because we lived in public, I would not alter my behavior or beliefs. And for this night, our kitchen table was in the middle of a Cracker Barrel restaurant. The next night it might be in a coffee shop in a motel, a four-star restaurant in a big city, or a truckstop in the middle of nowhere. We spent so much time on our bus, the Dreamchaser, out on life's highways, that it became

Our travels and misadventures are a story in itself!

Our bus driver Gaylon Moore showing band bus driver Ernie Stewart how much he'd just eaten

our home, the fans were our neighbors, and the concert stage was our living room. Wherever you go, there you are.

Who'da Thought?

In 1947, forty-three percent of families said grace aloud before family meals. By 1997, the percentage increased to sixty-three percent. There is hope! Ninety-four percent of all Americans believe in God or a universal spirit. I say if you don't, you're a few sandwiches short of your picnic.

Road Scholars

The school of hard knocks is always in session. There's homework, a final exam, and you never know when you're going to be surprised by a pop quiz. Experience is always the best teacher. Wy, Ashley, and I are road scholars.

Did you hear about the "dial-a-prayer" for atheists? Nobody answers the phone when you call.

The Girls Next Door

When Wynonna and I got to stay in one place for a whole week in Omaha, Nebraska in 1989, we'd gotten so tired of room service we chose to stay at the Residence Inn so we could have a kitchen to cook in. We pretended we were secretaries living in apartments. I called her Betty and she called me Norma Normal (the name I used to wrestle under). The first night, after our show, still in our outrageous stage outfits, we headed for the local supermarket with our grocery list at about one in the morning. The place was empty, except for a couple of cab drivers and the stock people sitting on the floor loading up the shelves. Here come Wy and I done up in our sparkly outfits, spike heels, and serious big hair, skipping as we pushed the carts through the aisles, merrily singing Judd songs. Such looks we got! One night I would make fried chicken and mashed potatoes with gravy, and invite "the neighbors" over. Then Wy—I mean Betty—would cook lasagne, and even our fanatically devoted road manager Mike McGrath (code name Aqua Boy) would dazzle us with macaroni and cheese and a fresh fruit salad sprinkled with shredded coconut. Happy days!

Macaroni and Cheese Casserole

If I were alone on a desert island, this is the one dish I would want to have.

MAKES 4 SERVINGS AS A MAIN DISH, OR 6 SERVINGS AS A SIDE DISH

8 ounces uncooked elbow macaroni or medium shells
½ stick or ¼ cup butter
¼ cup all-purpose flour
2 cups milk
6 ounces Velveeta or sharp Cheddar cheese, cut into small chunks, plus a little extra shredded for topping
Salt and pepper, to taste

1. Preheat the oven to 350°.

2. Cook the macaroni according to the package directions. Drain well.

3. Meanwhile, in a large, heavy saucepan, melt the butter. Whisk in the flour to make a paste. Gradually whisk in the milk. Bring to a simmer over medium heat, whisking, until thickened, about 1 minute. Add the cheese, salt, and pepper and whisk until smooth.

4. Stir the cooked macaroni into the cheese sauce. Scrape into a shallow 2-quart baking dish.

5. Bake in the 350° oven, uncovered, until bubbly and lightly golden on top, 20 to 25 minutes. Add the extra shredded cheese for the last 5 minutes of baking. Let stand 10 minutes before serving.

Blessed are they who can laugh at themselves, for they shall never cease to be amused.

My favorite part of playing at state fairs was the 4-H exhibits. Seeing those youngsters' sense of responsibility and creativity makes me feel better about our next generation. My second favorite part about state fairs was the corn dogs.

Corn Dogs

Plop me down in the middle of a state fair and I'll go running for the corn dogs every time. (Remember to wait one hour after eating before riding the roller coaster.) This is my Mom's version.

MAKES **8 TO 10 SERVINGS**

8 to 10 hot dogs, at room temperature, blotted dry with paper towels (we use turkey weiners)

BATTER

1 cup Bisquick
2 tablespoons white cornmeal
½ teaspoon dry mustard
¼ teaspoon paprika
⅛ teaspoon ground hot red pepper (cayenne)
1 large egg, lightly beaten
½ cup milk

About 6 cups vegetable oil (48-ounce bottle), for frying
Prepared yellow mustard, for spreading, and/or hot-pepper sauce, for sprinkling

1. Make sure the hot dogs are at room temperature.

2. *Make the batter:* In a large bowl, stir together the Bisquick, cornmeal, dry mustard, paprika, and red pepper. Stir in the egg and milk until well blended. Let the batter rest for 10 minutes.

3. Into a large (3-quart) saucepan, pour enough oil to come to a depth of about 2 inches. Heat over medium-high heat until the oil registers 370° on a deep-fat frying thermometer.

4. Dip a hot dog in the batter to thoroughly coat. Then with tongs, slip the dog into the hot oil—do 2 dogs at a time, no more. More than 2 will lower the temperature of the cooking oil. Cook the dogs, turning with a metal slotted spoon, until browned all over, 2 to 3 minutes. Remove the dogs to paper towels to drain. Repeat with the remaining dogs.

5. If you'd like, stick a wooden skewer in one end of each dog. Spread the outside with the prepared mustard and/or sprinkle with hot sauce.

Caught in the act at the Indiana State Fair in 1984

My Favorite Cheesecake

Eat it today, wear it tomorrow. On the road, I like to order cheesecake, 'cause I figure it's a safe bet—you can't mess it up too badly. Here's my recipe, with a sour cream topping. Of course cherries, blueberries, strawberries, and raspberries make a good second topping.

MAKES **10** SERVINGS

CRUST

½ **stick or ¼ cup butter**

1 **cup graham cracker crumbs**

FILLING

2 **packages (8 ounces each) cream cheese, at room temperature**

¾ **cup sugar**

4 **large eggs, separated**

1 **tablespoon fresh lemon juice**

2 **teaspoons pure vanilla extract**

TOPPING

1 **container (8 ounces) sour cream**

2 **tablespoons sugar**

1 **teaspoon vanilla extract**

1. Preheat the oven to 350°.

2. *Make the crust:* In a small saucepan, melt the butter. Stir in the crumbs to moisten. Press the crumbs in an even layer over the bottom of a 9-inch springform pan.

3. *Make the filling:* In a large bowl, with an electric mixer at medium speed, beat together the cream cheese and sugar until smooth. Add the yolks, beating thoroughly. Beat in the lemon juice and vanilla, blending well.

4. In a second clean large bowl, with clean beaters, beat the egg whites until stiff peaks form. With a rubber spatula, stir a little of the beaten whites into the cheese mixture to lighten. Gently fold in the remaining whites. Pour over the crust in the springform pan.

5. Bake in the 350° oven until the top center of the cake is set, 30 to 40 minutes.

6. *Make the topping:* In a small bowl, stir together the sour cream, sugar, and vanilla. Spread the topping over the cheesecake. Bake another 5 minutes. Let the cheesecake cool completely in the pan on a wire rack. Cover loosely and refrigerate for several hours until thoroughly chilled before serving.

7. To serve, remove the side of the pan.

Goals are dreams
with deadlines.

Dinner-table questions:
"What do you consider your
biggest accomplishment?
What are your goals? What
will it take to achieve them?"

WELCOME HOME

Nutrition is not just about feeding the body—it's the connection between the body, mind, and spirit. Starve one and the others suffer. We're not simple creatures who live by bread alone. When I return to my farm, Peaceful Valley, after a particularly hard trip on the road giving lectures, and I'm tired both physically and emotionally, I need to nourish myself. I believe your home should be a psychological fortress. If Larry is off on a trip and no one else is around except the four dogs, I call my housekeeper Dorthey and assistant Lynn and tell them to take the day off so I can be alone. Silence is refreshment for the soul. I may not talk to anyone for the whole day. I often go for a walk in the woods or lie outside in the hammock with Ramona, the floppy-eared stray who showed up at our barn one day. After I've reconnected with nature, I go back indoors to make my favorite sandwich, and slowly become one with myself again.

Get a hammock.

Naomi's Avocado Sandwich

Recently I visited with my girlfriend Jane Seymour on the set of her television show, "Dr. Quinn, Medicine Woman," and talked about the excitement of her being a new mom with twins, at mid-life. Since she shares my love of the avocado, especially in guacamole, I gave her this recipe.

- **2 slices whole-wheat bread**
- **2 tablespoons mayonnaise, or as much as you like**
- **6 slices avocado, tossed with a little fresh lemon juice**
- **⅓ cup sliced small, fresh mushrooms**
- **3 slices tomato**
- **3 tablespoons shredded mozzarella**
- **1 tablespoon sunflower seeds**

1. Preheat the broiler.

2. Spread one side of each bread slice with 1 tablespoon mayonnaise, or more. On one slice, layer the avocado, mushrooms, tomato, cheese, and sunflower seeds.

3. Broil the layered avocado half of the sandwich 4 to 6 inches from the heat until the cheese melts and the sunflower seeds are lightly toasted, 3 to 4 minutes. Top with the other slice of bread, cut the sandwich in half, and eat.

Silence Is Refreshment for the Soul

I'm not sure I agree with Ashley who fasts periodically, but I do go on a news fast regularly. I go several days without watching TV, reading the paper, listening to a radio or Barry Manilow records. (Hey, we once lived without a TV and a telephone for two years!) At our house we try not to watch violent or demeaning shows or buy products that sponsor them. TV lets people into your home you'd never invite over.

When I was eight, I remember Daddy bringing home our first TV. I thought it was going to be a Tell-a-Vision. Boy, have I been disappointed.

Now Starring: Geek Goddess

When Wynonna and Ashley return home from long concert tours or filming movies on location, they sometimes have what I call Road Rash, and are in much need of Mom's TLC. The best prescription for this irritable condition is Wy's beef stroganoff with yeast rolls on the side. One time while we were eating on the picnic table in the backyard, Wy and Ash weren't laughing at my jokes, so I quickly improvised and choreographed the Big Butt Dance. My inspiration came from what I call the butt-extender ingredients, or Fifth Food Group, in this meal—sour cream and butter for the rolls. I was wearing tights, so I dashed into the house, stuck two pillows down the back of my tights, raced back outside, and jumped up on the picnic table, where I began gyrating. Live entertainment for their dining pleasure!

Beef Stroganoff

In our house, we love anything with noodles. I like "cutting up" while I cut the steak up with a pair of cooking scissors—it makes the job a whole lot easier and more fun.

MAKES 4 SERVINGS

- 3 tablespoons vegetable oil
- 1 pound top round steak, trimmed of excess fat, cut into bite-size pieces
- 1 cup chopped onion
- 1 cup water
- ½ cup dry red wine (optional)
- ¼ cup Worcestershire sauce
- 2 cups sliced fresh mushrooms or 2 cans (7 ounces each) sliced mushrooms, drained
- 1 package (.75 ounce) brown-gravy mix
- 2 tablespoons all-purpose flour
- 4 ounces uncooked medium egg noodles (about 2½ cups)
- 1 container (8 ounces) sour cream
- ½ teaspoon salt

1. In a large, heavy skillet, heat the oil over medium-high heat. Add the meat and onion and sauté until the meat is browned and the onion is softened, about 3 minutes. Reduce the heat to low. Stir in the water, red wine, if using, Worcestershire sauce, and mushrooms. Cover the skillet and simmer until the meat is "fall apart" tender, about 45 minutes.

2. Push the meat to one side of the skillet and whisk in the gravy mix. Sprinkle with the flour and stir to mix. Simmer until thickened, about 1 minute. Keep warm over very low heat.

3. Meanwhile, in a large pot of boiling water, cook the noodles until tender, about 5 minutes. Drain the noodles.

4. Stir the sour cream and salt into the meat mixture. Gently heat through, stirring, but do not let the mixture even simmer or the sour cream will separate. Spoon over the cooked noodles and serve immediately.

If you dribble some food on yourself in a restaurant, ask for club soda right away. One of the best things to remove a grease spot is shampoo or dishwashing detergent. I've learned if a server at Red Lobster spills something on you, you get your meal free with the club soda.

I tell the girls being a success in a career isn't worth being a failure at home.

The Triangle at Trilogy

We owned and operated our own restaurant named Trilogy—which refers to three art forms closely related (get it? music, movies, books)—recognized as Nashville's best. Often when I was returning home from travels, I'd call our chef and order her specials. It's a long drive out to our rural farm, and since I've never cared for fast food or airplane food, I'm always starving at the end of a day of travel. My usual order would go something like this: grilled salmon, rice and glazed carrots, Caesar salad, and crème brûlée. I ordered huge adult bibs for the girls and myself through a mail-order catalogue. Ashley wears hers on a movie set when she's in costume and it's lunch break. Wy does the same thing if she's doing a photo session or a video. I keep mine in the glove box for eating in the car.

After Trilogy was named "Nashville's Best New Restaurant," we closed it. We had a family powwow, and the vote was unanimous: The restaurant was interfering with our family. For a year Larry had been there practically all the time. This is a perfect example of how strongly we feel about putting family above everything, even money! So the bad news is that we chose to close Nashville's most happening eatery. The good news is that Larry is going to be home for supper again and we can take our twilight walks.

Some of my favorite dishes at our restaurant were fettuccine with shrimp, roasted chicken, and a romaine salad with goat cheese and walnuts. Following are recipes for a few more of my favorites.

The country song lyric "Two things money can't buy . . . true love and home-grown tomatoes" pretty much sums it up. It's true money can't buy happiness, but I say it can help calm your nerves! It also works like manure—you gotta spread it around.

Know what a "meat and three" is? A restaurant where you order your entree and then select 3 side dishes from another column on the menu. There's one on Main Street in our hometown of Franklin, Tennessee, called Dotsons. A neon sign over the door bids: "Y'all C'mon In." They play country-music videos and the girls sing along as they serve. Be sure to check out Larry's fish on the wall if you go.

If Your Favorite Thing to Make for Dinner Is Reservations . . .

As a former restaurateur, may I suggest if there's ever a problem in a restaurant, always tell the manager—they want to know. Don't undertip your waiter or waitress just because the food is bad—they didn't cook it. But on the other hand, don't encourage bad service or attitudes by tipping the standard amount. It's not a bad idea to overtip your breakfast waitress, since their average customer check is small. Question: Why do you suppose women tip less than men?

Open Up Your Heart . . .

The number-one disease in our country is heart disease. Dr. Dean Ornish, the pioneering cardiologist, has proven that a program of meditation, group support, and a low-fat diet not only halts the progression of heart disease but actually can reverse it. No, this is not a misprint—it can actually halt and reverse it! Fifty million Americans, or one in four, have high blood pressure. It can lead to stroke, heart attack, or kidney failure. Did you ever stop to think that eighty-five percent of all illness is self-limiting? Most hospital patients are there because no one taught them healthy life-styles.

F.Y.I.: Almost nobody got cancer or heart disease before 1905. The first heart attack was described in the *Journal of the American Medical Association* in 1908. What do you think has happened?

Trilogy's Curried Lentils

The girls and I used to eat a lot of bean dishes in our tight-budget days. They are inexpensive and high in protein. Olive oil, a monounsaturated fat, has been shown to help prevent blood clots and the formation of arterial plaque. It's the oil of choice at our house for cooking just about everything, except popcorn. So, time to check your oil.

MAKES **8** SERVINGS

> **3 tablespoons olive oil**
> **2 cups brown lentils**
> **1 cup chopped onion**
> **3 tablespoons chopped garlic**
> **2 carrots, trimmed, quartered**
>   **lengthwise, and sliced**
> **3 tablespoons curry powder**
> **½ teaspoon ground cumin**
> **½ teaspoon chili powder**
> **¼ teaspoon salt**
> **2 cans (about 14 ounces each)**
>   **vegetable, chicken, or beef broth,**
>   **plus enough water to equal 4 cups**
> **1 tablespoon chopped fresh cilantro**

1. In a large Dutch oven, heat the oil over medium heat. Add the lentils and cook, stirring constantly, for 2 to 3 minutes. Add the onion, garlic, and carrot, and cook, stirring occasionally, until the vegetables begin to brown, about 5 minutes.

2. Stir in the curry, cumin, chili powder, and salt, and cook, stirring, for 1 to 2 minutes. Add the broth and water mixture. Bring to a simmer and then simmer, covered, over low heat until everything is tender and the flavors are blended, about 45 minutes.

3. To serve, stir in the cilantro.

Potato Fritters

These were created by Debra Desaulniers, the award-winning chef at Trilogy. Loosen your belt. Larry claims he's got Dunlop's disease—his belly's done lopped over his belt.

MAKES 4 SERVINGS
(12 FRITTERS)

2 heaping cups leftover mashed
   potatoes (or made fresh)
¼ cup finely chopped green bell
   pepper
¼ cup finely chopped onion
2 large eggs, lightly beaten
½ teaspoon salt
¼ teaspoon ground white pepper,
   or to taste
1 cup plain dry bread crumbs
Vegetable oil, for frying

1. In a large bowl, mix together the mashed potatoes, bell pepper, onion, eggs, salt, and white pepper. With a rubber spatula, fold in ½ cup of the bread crumbs.

2. Spread the remaining ½ cup of bread crumbs on a sheet of waxed paper.

3. Using a ¼ cup dry measure, shape potato mixture into 12 patties or fritters, about ¼- to ½-inch thick. Lightly coat the fritters with the crumbs on the waxed paper, and set aside.

4. Into a 3-quart saucepan, pour the oil to a depth of 1 inch. Heat the oil until it registers 375° on a deep-fat frying thermometer.

5. Working in batches, with a metal slotted spoon, slide in fritters and cook 2 to 3 minutes, turning over once, until golden. Transfer to paper towels to drain. Serve hot.

I remember seeing a sign above a clock in a cafe that said, "This clock will never be stolen. Too many employees are watching it!"

Tabouli with Sun-Dried Tomatoes

MAKES 6 SERVINGS

2¾ cups (16 ounces) uncooked bulghur
1 cup sun-dried tomatoes
2 cups boiling water
½ cup olive oil
¼ cup fresh lemon juice
2 small cloves garlic, finely chopped
1 cup chopped fresh parsley
½ cup chopped green onion
½ cup finely chopped fresh mint
1 teaspoon salt
¾ teaspoon black pepper
1 medium tomato, chopped
1 small cucumber, peeled, seeded,
   and chopped

1. Prepare the bulghur according to package directions.

2. In a small bowl, soak the sun-dried tomatoes in the hot water until softened, about 10 minutes. Drain and chop.

3. In a medium bowl, whisk the oil and lemon juice. Add the garlic, parsley, green onion, mint, salt, and pepper. Stir in the sun-dried tomatoes and bulghur. Cover and refrigerate overnight.

4. To serve, stir in the fresh tomato and cucumber.

Parmesan Poblano Cheese Grits

You won't need to eat again for three days! This one is from Trilogy. Grits are ground dried hominy. The early settlers named them "groats," but Southerners mispronounced them grits. "Jaeatjet?" Yankee translation: "Did you eat yet?"

MAKES 6 SERVINGS

    2 cups water
    ½ teaspoon salt
    ½ cup grits
    1 tablespoon finely chopped, seeded,
      fresh poblano chile
    ½ stick or ¼ cup butter
    1 cup grated Parmesan cheese
    ½ cup heavy cream
    ⅛ teaspoon white pepper

1. In a medium saucepan, bring the water and salt to a rolling boil. Slowly stir in the grits. Reduce the heat to low. Cover the pan and cook, stirring occasionally, until thickened and smooth, 15 to 20 minutes.

2. Stir in the chile, butter, cheese, cream, and white pepper. Bring to a simmer, and then simmer to blend flavors, 1 to 2 minutes. Serve immediately.

Wy says, "Singing puts grits in the pantry!"

SLOW DOWN AND SIMPLIFY: "MY CUP OF SOLITUDE"

*S*begin my day at home the same way—with a quiet ritual. After I awaken, I luxuriate in bed for about five minutes. Have you discovered flannel sheets and pillow cases for the winter months? I say thank you to God for allowing me to be here and for the potential of the new day. I don't think, "What do I have to do today?" I exclaim, "Great! What do I get to do today?" As soon as I get out of bed, I walk across my bedroom to a window that looks out on beautiful hills and rolling fields with horses and deer. I'm always struck by the timelessness of that landscape. I put on my favorite comfy robe and go downstairs to make coffee— flavored half decaf, half regular. Our four dogs are excited to see me and we all go outside. I do my yoga stretches and deep breathing, saluting the sun.

Here's a question for you: Do you say, "Good God, it's morning!" or "Good morning, God!"?

"I resign as manager of the Universe."

Solitude is creativity's best friend.

Serve up some Food for Thought during a family meal: "What is your idea of perfect happiness? Of what are you most afraid?"

I go back in, turn on my instrumental imagination music, and ceremoniously enjoy my coffee in a special cup—I have one for each season. Relaxing at the kitchen table with my cup of solitude, I consider how I want the day to go. It's during this quiet time that I organize the day, the week, and sometimes even the month.

So I choose to start each new day with God, gratitude, animals, nature, sensory pleasures such as stretching, breathing, and music, and a sense of being in control of my life. I would no more not start my day like this than I would walk out of my house without clothes on (or as we hillbillies say, "necked").

Naomi's Smoothie Shake

I can make this shake very quickly and take it with me out onto my deck for a quiet break. Sometimes, I'll pour it into a large thermal cup or mug that I've first stored in the freezer to get it good and cold—that way the shake stays colder longer. This is one of my favorite things to have in the car on the way to the airport when I'm leaving town.

Yogurt helps replace any loss of beneficial bacteria in your digestive tract, so it's a good idea to eat yogurt if you're on antibiotics, because medicine often destroys all bacteria equally—even the good group. It's also easy to make. You can get a yogurt maker at your favorite health-food store.

MAKES 2 SERVINGS

- 1 container (16 ounces) low-fat plain yogurt
- 1 banana, sliced
- 1 heaping cup fresh or frozen strawberries, hulled, or peach slices or other fruit

Combine all the ingredients in a blender and blend until smooth, and then pour into a tall glass over ice, if you'd like.

The Power of Your Plate

If you're prone to eating when you're on an emotional roller coaster, have a sweet—no fruit—or starchy snack. For those really stressful times, eat something high in carbohydrates and low in protein, like the potato fritters (page 68). These foods stimulate the release of a neurohormone called serotonin in the brain, which helps calm the mind and therefore the body. I love popcorn—it has the same effect. My sis Margaret and I make it almost every night before bedtime. Her pet name is even "Popcorn." She says one day they'll discover the popcorn gene.

Rest Is an Overlooked Priority

My best bedtime sedative is first to dim the lights one hour before sleep to start the release of natural melatonin, and then take a long hot bath surrounded by scented candles. I slip into bed and sip a cup of valerian root tea, or 1 teaspoon tincture of valerian in an ounce or two of water. Larry and I never go to sleep without settling an argument, if we've had one, and we have learned never to discuss anything upsetting after 8 p.m. If I'm in a hotel, I use ear plugs and a sleep mask. I also use a night light in the hotel bathroom ever since that time I groggily woke up in the middle of the night and stepped out into the hallway by mistake, and the door locked behind me.

Husband, dogs, popcorn—perfect harmony

Being in the Moment

Part of slowing down is putting all your attention into the moment. I take walks in the afternoon when I'm out on the road, wandering through neighborhoods, talking to shopkeepers and everyday folks I run into on the street. When I'm home, I stroll through the valley in the evenings, practicing mindfulness and listening to my inner stirrings. To be able to fully enjoy awareness of the *present* moment is truly a gift—a *present!* My favorite time of day is the period between sunset and darkness, that half-in-between state of dusk or twilight. It's called liminality, the state between, where the usual rules don't apply. I've never liked rules anyway.

Living in the Moment

When I suggested to pop superstar Michael Bolton that he write a duet with Wynonna, he eagerly accepted my offer to visit the farm. We were relaxing out in the backyard after a delicious vegetarian meal. It was that time of day when liminality rules. Michael was listing all the things that were coming up for him: learning Italian to tour with Luciano Pavarotti and Placido Domingo, writing a movie screenplay, working on a children's book, writing songs and recording, and spending time with his three daughters. I just nodded silently and then finally inquired, "Michael, what are you feeling right this moment?" He was sitting there in a lawn chair under a walnut tree in the beautiful fading light, licking a grape Popsicle. I wondered out loud, "Are you really _tasting_ that?" He stopped and

Gyms with loud music where people on metal equipment look at themselves in mirrors aren't for me.

sighed, and his shoulders visibly slumped, as he looked at the Popsicle with new eyes. Michael, who's very intelligent, had suddenly shifted gears. "What do you _see_?" I asked next. As he looked over toward the field, a blanket of fireflies magically rose up out of the ground. "Wow, look at that!" he murmured. One of the dogs was lying on his feet, and he bent over to stroke her, then slipped off his shoes. He began rubbing his bare feet in the thick grass and let out a sigh. "Ohhh . . . that _feels_ good." I watched Michael cock his head as he _listened_ to the silence for the first time. "Can you just shut down the outside world for a moment and be here, in Peaceful Valley? Can you really be a human be-ing, not a human do-ing? Take some deep breaths," I encouraged. "What's that wonderful _smell_?" he asked. The air was fragrant with honeysuckle. Michael comfortably sank down in his chair, stretching his legs out and letting his arms fall over the armrests. It was such a transformation. He beamed serenity.

Most of us miss out on those public prizes—the Pulitzer, the Nobel, the Oscar, the Tony, the Emmy, and the Grammy. But we can all win those important prizes— a great meal, friendship, a crackling fire, a gorgeous sunset, and a good book.

Wy and her other partner

Tension is who you think you should be. Relaxation is who you really are.

Michael Bolton's Marinara Sauce

When visiting our house, Michael's favorite thing is riding a four-wheeler through the woods. His other favorite thing is this meal. You can also toss some cut-up grilled vegetables into the sauce.

MAKES ENOUGH FOR 8 TO 10 SERVINGS

¾ **cup olive oil**
4 **cups coarsely chopped onion**
4 **tablespoons finely chopped garlic**
8 **cups pureed fresh tomatoes,**
    or 3 cans (29 ounces each) whole
    tomatoes, drained, and pureed
2½ **teaspoons salt**
1 **teaspoon ground black pepper**
¼ **cup chopped fresh oregano**
    or 1 tablespoon dried oregano
⅓ **cup chopped fresh basil**
    or 1 tablespoon dried basil

1. In a large, heavy saucepan, heat the oil over medium heat. Add the onion and garlic and cook until the onion is soft-ened, about 10 minutes. Add the tomatoes, 2 teaspoons of the salt, and the pepper. If using dried herbs, add them now. Simmer, partially covered, for 30 minutes or until very thick.

2. Very carefully, and working in batches, puree the mixture in a food processor or blender. Return to the saucepan. If using fresh herbs, add them now along with the remaining salt, and then con-tinue to simmer, partially covered, for another 30 minutes or until as thick as you like. Serve over penne or other favorite shaped pasta, figuring about 3 to 4 ounces of uncooked pasta per serving.

A relaxing suppertime at Peaceful Valley

In today's world, we know more but care less. Seems the experts have more and more information to give people who have less and less time to be paying attention.

Get a bird feeder. I love to watch the hummingbirds out my kitchen window.

Grilled Vegetable Salad, Hot and Cold

This is based on a salad I get at my favorite restaurant in L.A., the Ivy. Ashley used to be the hostess there. It's such an "in" place, even the servers must have appeared in at least two major films! Your favorite movie stars are probably eating there right now! We had this salad when Michael Bolton came to dinner at Peaceful Valley.

MAKES 4 SERVINGS

DRESSING

1 cup olive oil
½ cup fresh lemon juice
¾ teaspoon sugar
2 tablespoons chopped fresh basil
½ teaspoon salt
¼ teaspoon cracked black pepper

SALAD

1 zucchini, trimmed and cut into ¾-inch dice
1 red bell pepper, stemmed, seeded, and cut into squares
1 yellow bell pepper, stemmed, seeded, and cut into squares
Fresh corn kernels scraped from 2 ears
1 cup diced eggplant
6 stalks of asparagus, trimmed and cut into bite-size pieces
3 teaspoons olive oil
¼ teaspoon salt
4 cups mixed torn lettuce leaves— we use several types combined
1 medium tomato, diced
1 avocado, peeled, pitted, and sliced
1 pound grilled shrimp or chicken (optional)

1. Prepare a grill with medium-hot coals or preheat the broiler.

2. *Make the dressing:* In a small bowl, whisk together the oil, lemon juice, sugar, basil, salt, and pepper. Refrigerate 30 minutes.

3. *Make the salad:* Create a basket by folding up the edges of a piece of heavy-duty aluminum foil. In a medium bowl, combine the zucchini, red and yellow bell peppers, corn, eggplant, and asparagus. Add the oil and toss to coat. Spoon the vegetables into the foil basket.

4. Place the basket on the grill and cover the grill, or place 5 inches from broiler. Cook, stirring occasionally, just until slightly tender, about 15 minutes. Season with the ¼ teaspoon salt.

5. Arrange the lettuce leaves in individual serving bowls. Place the tomatoes and avocado slices on top. Add the vegetables and the shrimp or chicken, if using, either still hot or at room temperature. Whisk the dressing again and pass at the table.

If you were guaranteed honest responses to any three questions, who would you question and what would you ask? Why?

Sweet Loretta Lynn confided to me once: "Sometimes it's like you're a big pie settin' on the table, and everybody runs up and gets their piece of you. When it's over, the plate's empty with only a few crumbs left."

A Stove, Refrigerator, Coffeemaker . . .

A friend of mine asked her elderly grandmother, if she could have only one modern convenience in her kitchen, what would it be? Grandmother's sobering reply? "Running water!" Speaking of running water . . . Don't forget to wash your hands well before you prepare food, and to scrub counter surfaces, especially after contact with raw meat. Only seventy-four percent of women wash their hands after using the bathroom, and only sixty-one percent of men. Mom will tell you, "Wash your hands and say your prayers, 'cause God and germs might be invisible—but they're everywhere!" She says cleanliness is next to Godliness, but it's not. I looked it up. It's next to some kind of succulent plant called claytonia.

Prioritism: Honesty, Realism, Organization

Make a decision to simplify your life, and the rest will follow—pun intended! Here are some of the things I have done, starting with the most important: prioritizing. Since we women are the care givers, it's hard for us to insist on personal time 'cause it makes us feel selfish. Wrong! You deserve it, because this is your health and sanity we are talking about.

This next statement may seem "not-so-nice," but I feel it's necessary to be truly honest with you. I reserve what little spare time I have for only those friends who are very special, and with whom I have a deep personal history or real connection. For me, it is more satisfying to have a few close and intimate relationships than to have several superficial or distant ones. Quality versus quantity!

I have also learned the hard way to be realistic when organizing my schedule and now know when to say "no." The word was not in my vocabulary until seven years ago, when I was diagnosed with a chronic disease. This wake-up call really caused me to sort through things and make adjustments.

Just a few of the everyday things I have done to simplify my life include canceling junk mail and magazine subscriptions I never read, buying clothes that are wash-and-wear and don't need dry cleaning or ironing, cleaning out drawers and closets and giving away items I never use or wear, and more important, delegating tasks that I would normally pile on my "to do" list. I sometimes even leave a message on my answering machine stating, "You're welcome to leave a message, but today is 'Be Kind to Me Day' and I am only returning emergency calls."

Most people spend their entire lives trying to learn about themselves. In a way, I have been fortunate—I was forced to come face-to-face with myself and make changes accordingly.

Don't surrender your sanity to someone else's insanity.

Blackberry Cobbler

I keep grapes, apples, bananas, and raisins (no fat and no cholesterol) around for in-between-meal snacks to keep me from eating all those darn Tootsie rolls.

During the summer, when the fruit is at its best, we like to eat a lot of cobblers. This is based on a favorite recipe from Choices, one of our local restaurants in Franklin, Tennessee. Can somebody out there please explain to me why a blackberry is red when it's green? It's keeping me up nights.

MAKES 8 SERVINGS

FILLING

  2 cups water
  1 cup sugar
  ¼ cup cornstarch
  6 cups fresh or frozen blackberries (see Note below)
  ½ stick or ¼ cup butter, cut up

CRUST

  1 cup sifted all-purpose flour
  ½ teaspoon salt
  ¼ cup vegetable oil
  2 tablespoons cold milk
  1 tablespoon butter, melted
  1 tablespoon sugar
  Vanilla ice cream (optional)

1. Preheat oven to 375°.

2. *Make the filling:* In a large saucepan, combine 1½ cups water and the sugar. Bring to a boil. Meanwhile, in a small bowl, stir together the cornstarch and remaining ½ cup water until smooth. Stir into the boiling water mixture. Return to the boil, stirring constantly. Reduce the heat and simmer until thickened, about 1 minute. Remove from the heat and stir in the berries and butter until the butter melts. Pour the filling into a 9 × 9 × 2-inch baking pan.

3. *Make the crust:* In a medium bowl, stir together the flour and salt. Add the oil and milk and stir until the dough comes together. Press into a ball. On a lightly floured surface, roll out the dough into a square to fit into the baking pan. If the crust cracks, just patch it together with your fingers. Place the dough over the filling. Brush with the melted butter and sprinkle with the sugar.

4. Bake in the 375° oven until the top is browned and the fruit filling is bubbly, about 40 minutes. Let cool on a wire rack. Serve warm in bowls with vanilla ice cream, if you'd like.

NOTE

If using frozen blackberries, partially thaw before using.

"*May beauty reign here, and lovely objects renew us by their silence and perfection.*"

—FROM *A HOUSE BLESSING*,
BY WELLERAN POLTARNESS

Rhubarb Cobbler

Serve the cobbler warm with a bowl of whipped cream on the side, or plop a scoop of ice cream on each serving.

MAKES 6 SERVINGS

FILLING

6 cups 1-inch pieces fresh rhubarb or frozen, thawed

¾ cup sugar, or more depending on tartness of rhubarb

⅛ teaspoon ground cinnamon

⅛ teaspoon ground ginger

6 tablespoons water

2 tablespoons cornstarch

TOPPING

1 cup all-purpose flour

1½ teaspoons baking powder

¼ teaspoon salt

⅓ cup skim milk

3 tablespoons vegetable oil

1. Preheat the oven to 400°.

2. *Make the filling:* In a medium, heavy saucepan, stir together the rhubarb, sugar, cinnamon, ginger, water, and cornstarch. Bring to a boil, stirring constantly. Boil, stirring, 1 minute. Pour into a 9 × 9 × 2-inch baking dish.

3. *Make the topping:* In a medium bowl, stir together the flour, baking powder, and salt. Stir in the milk and oil. Work the mixture in the bowl with your hands to make a dough. Pull off pieces of dough, about 2 tablespoons each, and shape into rounds about 2 inches in diameter, and place over the top of the fruit mixture.

4. Bake in the 400° oven until the filling is bubbly and the topping is golden brown, 25 to 30 minutes. Serve warm.

Can anyone explain this to me: Since so many people place great emphasis on a happy private life, why do you think they spend more time and energy on their professional lives?

Orange Ice

Or, how to register a 10 on the emotional Richter Scale. After my grandson Elijah Judd Kelley and I come in from seeing who can get the dirtiest playing outside, I hand him one of my homemade orange ice Popsicles, and he kisses me on the cheek, squealing, "Love you, Mamaw."

MAKES 8 SERVINGS

4 cups water

2 cups sugar

2 cups fresh orange juice (or from a carton)

¼ cup fresh lemon juice

1. In a medium, heavy saucepan, stir together the water and sugar. Bring to a boil and gently boil for 15 minutes. Remove from the heat and let cool.

2. Add the orange juice and lemon juice.

3. Pour into a 13 × 9 × 2-inch metal pan. (Or pour into ice cube trays and add wooden Popsicle sticks.) Place in the freezer until mixture begins to freeze around the edges, about 1½ hours. Stir the edges into the center of the ice. Return to freezer and freeze until solid, about 2 hours.

4. To serve, scoop ice into fancy dessert glasses or hollowed-out orange halves.

When Elijah gets his homemade Popsicle, he climbs up on the picnic table and dances a jig.

To Each His Zone

If your family is like ours, stress is an omnipresent problem. So it's important that we create zones of comfort and security within our lives. We need to book time for hobbies and other outlets for relaxation just as we schedule any other appointments, remembering that the word "recreation" comes from "re-create."

Stress takes an incredible toll on our minds, and therefore on our bodies. Bet you didn't know that more heart attacks happen on Monday mornings at nine o'clock than at any other time and that the number-one indicator for a heart attack is job dissatisfaction.

Eighty-five percent of all illness can be directly related to unresolved stress. If you don't acknowledge what's going on in your life, your body takes over. In 1997, the World Health Organizaton declared stress the number-one health problem.

Larry's Spaghetti Sauce

When Larry wants to unwind, he goes into our kitchen and makes his favorite spaghetti sauce. His motto is "Real men use garlic." This humble bulb is so good for us—it has antibiotic properties (allicin) and can help lower cholesterol in the blood. Serve the sauce over spaghetti or a shaped pasta like penne, ziti, or rotelle.

MAKES ENOUGH FOR 10 SERVINGS (FIGURING ABOUT 4 OUNCES OR SO OF PASTA PER SERVING)

1 pound ground beef round

8 cloves garlic, finely chopped, or 1½ teaspoons garlic powder

3 cans (14½ ounces each) stewed tomatoes

2 cans (6 ounces each) tomato paste

1 small green bell pepper, stemmed, seeded, and diced

1½ teaspoons dried Italian seasoning

1 teaspoon garlic salt

1 bay leaf

⅛ teaspoon ground hot red pepper (optional)

Garlic Bread (opposite page)

1. In a large saucepan, sauté the beef over medium heat, working in batches if necessary, until no longer pink, about 6 to 8 minutes. If using fresh garlic, add along with the meat. Drain the excess fat from the meat.

2. Stir in the stewed tomatoes, tomato paste, green pepper, Italian seasoning, garlic salt (and the garlic powder, if not using the fresh garlic above), bay leaf,

and hot red pepper, if using. Simmer over very low heat, partially covered, stirring occasionally, for 1½ hours or until it reaches desired consistency. Remove the bay leaf and serve the sauce over spaghetti, with Garlic Bread on the side.

Garlic Bread

MAKES ABOUT 6 SERVINGS, AND KEEPS THE VAMPIRES AWAY.

1 loaf Italian or French bread, sliced or cut horizontally in half, or 6 hamburger buns, split
½ stick or ¼ cup butter, at room temperature
1 teaspoon garlic powder

Preheat the broiler. Spread the cut sides of the bread with butter. Sprinkle with garlic powder. Broil about 4 inches from the heat until the butter is melted and the edges of the bread are crisp.

My husband Larry has his favorite stress-busters—working with his horses, fishing in our lake, and riding his Harley with Wy or me. And then there's cooking.

Home Ec for Men

I was feeling envious that our friend Guy learned to cook, do the laundry, and perform other household chores when his wife Angie went out of town for a month. When I told Larry about this and asked what he'd do if I was gone that long, he quickly replied, "Go over to Guy's house."

TIMES OF SICKNESS AND HEALTH

How I Almost Bought the Farm

You may ask, "Why this section in a cookbook?" These are my "recipes" for dealing with illness in my own life, and I want to share them with you.

Soon after I was diagnosed with hepatitis C in 1990, I had to announce my retirement from country music, but certainly not my retirement from life. Of the five forms of viral hepatitis—A through E—hepatitis C is the most dangerous. More than four million Americans have hepatitis C, and more than 30,000 are newly infected with it every year. Although it is a major health problem, little money has gone into research and not much is known about the disease. Hepatitis C has been overlooked and misunderstood because it's been given no media attention, and there is still no cure. For seven years I have been active in finding solutions by using both conventional medicine and complementary methods. I have been engaged in a voyage of self-discovery on a journey to wholeness. I've started the Naomi Judd Education and Research Fund, which works with the American Liver Foundation. For information about the disease and the fund and how to make a contribution, call 1-800-223-0179.

Throughout life and its many obstacles, we need to step out of our circumstances and live in hope. Hope helps us cope! It helps keep us from sinking in our fears

When folks would ask me what I was going to do when I quit singing, I'd tell them I planned to turn my garage into a beauty shop!

and propels us beyond our doubts. I tell people I counsel, who have incurable "problems," to list the killer diseases that seemed unconquerable at the turn of the century. They name typhoid fever, polio, and malaria, among others, all of which are unheard of anymore in this country. Then I reassure them that scientists or doctors may find cures for their diseases any day, just as early researchers discovered miracle drugs for other once-deadly infections.

My work with cancer and AIDS patients has taught me about the important difference between healing and curing. There's not always a cure, but there can always be healing. Peace isn't the absense of a disease, a conflict, or a problem— it's the ability to deal with it. And peace of mind is the goal.

Life Is Short, but It's Wide

We've learned there are eight things people who survive serious illness all seem to have in common. These are the eight ingredients to not just survive but to thrive:

1. Faith: There is now documented evidence that having religious beliefs improves health. (Scientific theories abound about why this is so.)

Visiting folks in the hospital is an important part of my life.

News flash: Change, challenge, and disappointment are part of life. (Pain is necessary, suffering is optional.)

Pieces of quiet

2. Support: A 1989 hallmark study by Dr. David Spiegel of eighty-six women with advanced cancer verified that women in support groups lived on the average more than eighteen months longer.

3. Humor: This boosts our immune functions, relaxes us, makes us more flexible, and gives us a sense of control.

4. Connecting with Nature: Modern life and technology have separated us from being outdoors, and being in nature is a great de-stresser.

5. Goals and Purposes: These keep us going by helping us focus on something positive and constructive. For me, educating others and working to find a cure for hepatitis C helps turn something negative into something positive, too.

6. Diet: Read this book.

7. Exercise: Gotta do it.

8. Open Belief System: Ah-ha! Very interesting—like the methods that help decrease stress. This just means being willing to consider all sorts of alternative methods for healing and curing.

If you're interested in learning more on the subject, my "sisterfriend" biochemist Candace Pert, Ph.D., just wrote a book called *Molecules of Emotion*. After all, every time you have a thought or emotion, a biochemical molecule (neuropepticle) is created. The brain is a lab of pharmaceuticals. Dr. Blair Justice,

Ph.D., a psychologist I know, wrote the first book I read on the subject, *Who Gets Sick*, and more recently, *How the Sick Stay Well*. There are great books out now that can change your life!

Looking for Dr. Right

Doctors aren't deities. Get referrals from friends and interview the prospective doctor. Trust your instincts. Look for one who cares about you as a person—a *person* with a problem. She or he should see themselves as partners with you in the healing journey.

Seeing double: Find two of them, 'cause a second opinion is even better. And remember, even two Dr. Rights can have a wrong opinion. Diagnosis and prognosis are just opinions.

The average doctor interrupts you after fourteen seconds, or two and a half sentences. When I was a nurse, I learned how important the caring aspect is, in addition to doing all the other technical things required of a nurse. My personal approach was to pull up a chair and listen carefully to each word a patient had to say. Listening is a fine art. The patient cares about how much you know, but needs to know how much you care!

You know you've met Dr. Wrong if he or she:

- *Repeatedly asks, "What's this red stuff?"*
- *Giggles when examining you.*
- *Offers to paint your car for $50.*
- *Tells you you're not getting enough fudge in your diet.*

Yoga is not a religion—it's a calming form of stretching.

For Women Only

Do you know the leading cancers in women? Lung, breast, colon/rectal, pancreatic, and ovarian, in that order. Some studies show that women between the ages of twenty-one and twenty-eight who exercise regularly cut their risk of breast cancer in half and reduce their chance of all types of cancer affecting the reproductive system. And by the way, it's a good idea to drink eight glasses of H_2O a day—a water purifier is worth the dollars. Since 1970, more than six hundred outbreaks of diseases caused by contaminated tap water have been reported to the U.S. Environmental Protection Agency. That's only a fraction of the incidents that really happen!

If you're planning to exercise, you need to replace fluid lost in perspiration, so try to drink two to three 8-ounce glasses two hours before exercising, one or two glasses five to ten minutes before, and then one glass every twenty minutes while exercising.

For Men Only

Cancer is a big killer in men, starting with cancer of the lung, prostate, colon/rectal, pancreas, and leukemia. Recent studies have indicated that tomatoes may help lessen men's risk of prostate cancer. But the single most important dietary step you can take for prostate cancer is to lower fat and calories in your diet. If you consume a lot of red meat, consider eliminating or greatly reducing the amount. A 9- to 14-ounce piece of prime rib can check in at 1,200 calories and 50 grams of fat! Men over fifty: Be sure to get the blood test (PSA) to check for prostate problems. I'm proud of my friend Mike Milken—yes, the former Junk Bond King—for starting and funding CAPCURE, the organization to fight this killer. For information, call 1-800-757-2873.

Life's Shock Absorber

Perhaps laughter is to the soul what soap is to the body. And I've seen that the shortest distance between two people is laughter. In our family we love to laugh. I said to Wynonna, "Laughter is like internal jogging," and she fired back, "Well, Mama, we ought to be in great shape!" Laughter's positive effects have been well documented. It increases immune-system activity and decreases stress hormones. I carry a whoopee cushion with me on the road and have even "gotten" the heads of the C.I.A., Judge William Webster, and the Hon. James Woolsey. No one is safe from my practical jokes!

Preschoolers laugh about four hundred times a day, while the average adult laughs fifteen—unless you're a Judd or around a Judd.

When Wy and I got to be clowns in the circus, we fulfilled fantasies of clobbering each other with pies.

A merry heart doeth good like a medicine.

—PROVERBS 17:22

Oliver Wendell Holmes said,
"One way to live a long life is
to acquire a chronic illness,
so you have to take good care
of yourself."

Uncommon Remedies for Common Concerns

- Echinacea, vitamin C, garlic, and ginger and zinc lozenges help ward off and lessen an already-caught cold or flu.

- The herb feverfew is great for preventing migraine headaches. Twenty-three million people suffer from migraines triggered by weather, bright light, food allergies, strong odors, stress, and menses. Take two or three fresh feverfew leaves, or 50 to 120 milligrams in pill form, daily.

- Fresh parsley fights bad breath.

- Peppermint minimizes gas.

- Chamomile soothes indigestion.

- Aloe vera salve relieves some skin problems.

- Dong quai is a plant in the carrot family that in some cases may ease the symptoms of menstruation and menopause.

- For my particular condition, I take milk thistle (silymarin) as a liver cleanser.

- To change an ex-boyfriend or husband into a Keebler elf . . . still working on it!

- Two teas for twin treatments: Green tea contains antioxidants that may deter tumor growth, but it also has caffeine. Ginseng—in tea, capsule, or even powder form—boosts energy and is thought to enhance the effectiveness of a low-fat diet in reducing cholesterol.

- Soybean products are gaining in popularity as a substitute for meat protein. Studies also show that a macrobiotic diet—low-fat, whole-grain, and organic—combats disease and can extend the life of cancer patients. This diet takes discipline, though!

We're learning more every day about the benefits of the phytochemicals found in plants. Herbal medicines can be tricky, however. You need to know what you are doing, because they can be potent! If you have a medical problem, seek professional medical advice, and investigate herbs thoroughly before taking them. Some products sold in health-food stores are worthless. Watch out for claims such as "miracle" or "amazing." You must educate yourself and take responsibility for your well-being!

Ready for a Change? We put a man on the moon in 1969, and invented shampoo and conditioner in one. Why don't we know more about hormone replacement therapy?

Chicken Soup to Make Your Cold Flu the Coop

All the great religious teachers of history have been saying the same three things: (1) go within and discover yourself; (2) do good to others; and (3) there's a higher power who loves you.

Chicken soup, affectionately known as Jewish penicillin, affects us on all three levels: the body, mind, and spirit. It tastes good and provides nutrients to the body; it awakens pleasing memories in the mind. And the act of receiving the soup from a loved one soothes the spirit, since it is a statement of love and compassion. Don't forget to have those zinc throat lozenges and echinacea for dessert.

MAKES 8 SERVINGS

4 cans (13¾ ounces each) chicken broth

6 large chicken breast halves, on the bone with skin (about 12 ounces each)

2 large onions, chopped

1 tablespoon dried marjoram

1 tablespoon dried basil

1 tablespoon chopped fresh cilantro

¾ teaspoon salt

1 teaspoon black pepper

3 carrots, trimmed and sliced

3 stalks celery, trimmed and sliced

1 can (16 ounces) lima beans, drained

1 package (16 ounces) egg noodles

1. In a large pot, combine the chicken broth, chicken breasts, and half the chopped onion. Bring to boiling. Add the marjoram, basil, cilantro, salt, and pepper. Simmer, partially covered, until chicken is tender and no longer pink near bone, about 30 minutes.

2. With slotted spoon, remove chicken from pot. When cool enough to handle, remove skin and bones and discard. Tear chicken into bite-size pieces. Return to pot. Add remaining onion, the carrot, and celery. Simmer, partially covered, until vegetables are tender, about 7 minutes. Add the lima beans and noodles. Simmer, covered, until noodles are tender, 15 to 17 minutes, stirring occasionally. Spoon into large soup bowls. (For a thinner soup, add more chicken broth.)

Help Yourself by Helping Yourself to a Supplement

Our bodies don't make vitamins, so we must obtain them from vegetables and fruit. And if our daily diet is not quite what it should be, or we have a medical problem, then supplements are a good idea. However, some people don't realize vitamin and mineral supplements are not meant to be a substitute for food—supplements should be taken *with* food.

I take all the antioxidants, mixed carotenoids, and selenium. A recent large-scale trial shows selenium can reduce the risk of cancer. Antioxidants are vitamins, minerals, and biochemicals that prevent damage to cells by substances called free radicals, which include pollutants and other toxic by-products of our industrial society.

I also take vitamins B, C, and E every day along with minerals such as zinc, calcium, and magnesium. If you have a specific health problem, first seek medical advice. Always keep in mind that too large a quantity of vitamin and mineral supplements can be harmful.

Here's one more thing to think about: Iron-containing supplements and medicines (even quit-smoking patches) are the number-one cause of accidental pediatric poisoning. Please childproof your house.

Don't be called out on strikes—go down swinging. Remember, you haven't failed until you've quit.

Both Are Better:
Stir Together and Mix Well

Just as side dishes complement the main entree, so complementary medical approaches can work hand-in-hand with conventional medicine. I prefer the word "complementary" to "alternative," so it doesn't imply these techniques are to be used instead of orthodox medical treatments.

As an R.N., I obviously believe in modern medicine. When it comes to surgery and fighting infections, we're the best. But people are becoming increasingly dissatisfied with the impersonal nature of the health-care industry, its inability to help chronic problems, and its cost—and with good reason!

Ever notice the first question you're asked: "Who's your insurance carrier?" In holistic medicine, the question is, "How can we help?" It's called holistic because it takes into consideration the whole person: body, mind, and spirit. It also focuses on prevention. Remember how I started this chapter? It realizes the importance of life-styles, environment, spirituality, and other influences in our lives that can't be measured by lab tests. The most popular holistic practices are massage and chiropractic and relaxation techniques. There's imagery, biofeedback, visualization, acupuncture, music, meditation and prayer, aromatherapy, hypnotherapy, and yoga. Most of these methods are as old as the Bible. And remember, what we call complementary medicine in this country is standard procedure for eighty percent of the rest of the world.

Once a nurse, always a nurse. We have three doctors: our spirit, mind, and body.

Why is complementary medicine growing? 'Cause it works! In 1993 the *Journal of the American Medical Association* reported that one out of every three of us use these methods and that together we are spending more than $14 billion a year on them. More than 125 medical schools, including Harvard, Yale, and Johns Hopkins, are offering courses in complementary medicine. Even the American Medical Association passed a resolution in 1996 stating their 300,000 members should "become better informed regarding the practices and techniques of alternative and unconventional medicine." It's the exciting frontier for anyone going into medicine.

Shift Your Gears

Sis Margaret and daughter Wy (and daughter Ashley, not pictured) are my best friends.

Vacations are very important stress-relievers, even if just for a long weekend. Getting away from your daily routine can improve your internal landscape and boost your immune system. Once a year, my sister Margaret and I take a sisterhood trip together. Did you ever consider that your sibling relationships are the longest you'll have?

It's so important that parents give their children equal amounts of love and attention. M.I.T.'s Frank Sulloway, Ph.D., recently suggested in his landmark book *Born To Rebel* that order of birth plays a major role in determining personality. When I questioned Frank about it, he responded, "Our personality is the repertoire of strategies that siblings use to compete with one another, secure their place in the family, and survive the ordeal of childhood."

Vegetable and Barley Soup-Stew

In addition to being restorative and healing, this thick vegetarian soup also makes a great party soup served with a big pan of fried corn cakes on a cold winter evening. We serve it at nighttime bonfires after hayrides in the valley. I like dishes I can make the day before, and this one tastes even better the next day.

MAKES 4 SERVINGS

1 zucchini, trimmed and cut into bite-size pieces

3 carrots, trimmed and sliced

3 stalks celery, trimmed and sliced

1 cup green peas, fresh or frozen

1 cup corn kernels, fresh or frozen

1 large onion, chopped

1 cup uncooked fine barley

2 cans (16 ounces each) stewed tomatoes

1 can (28 ounces) tomato juice

¼ teaspoon pepper

1 bay leaf

In a large pot, combine all the ingredients. Bring to boiling over high heat. Let boil for 10 minutes. Reduce the heat to low. Cover and cook, stirring often, until all the vegetables are tender, about 1 hour. Remove the bay leaf before serving.

Every spring, Mark baptizes folks in a beautiful creek near his church.

Wy holding cousin Brian, Mom, Mark, Middy, me, and Larry

DINNER ON THE GROUND

My younger brother Mark pastors a hundred-year-old white-frame Baptist church on a one-lane road in Colesburg, Kentucky. When spring brings warm weather, he baptizes people in the creek and holds fellowship dinners with his congregation. Sometimes these community dinners are picnics outside, in that Southern tradition called "dinner on the ground."

Grow Your Own

Our Judd ancestors were farmers, and now Mark still raises a big garden every year in his backyard. His seven-year-old son Brian (a.k.a. Sweetie Pie) likes to warn me, "Watch what you say in the garden, Aunt Naomi, 'cause the corn has ears!"

Daddy raised radishes in the dirt plot in front of his gas station, and Mom had tomato plants by her rosebushes off our back porch. Sister Margaret enjoys the exercise she gets from doing all her own yard work. Ashley has an incredible green thumb for flowers and gardening, and Wy and I are into organic farming. Since we have so little time to maintain what we plant, someone who doesn't use pesticides and chemicals oversees this for us. When I have to buy produce at the grocery, I get the organically grown kind, even though it costs more. Next time you get ready to eat an apple, scrape the wax off the skin and you'll understand!

Even if you live in an apartment, you might consider planting flowers, or herbs and spices, in a window box. Growing marijuana is illegal.

Ashley, cousin Erin, and Wy buying vegetables in Morrill, Kentucky

Buy veggies and fruit from farm stands and trucks with folks who advertise with hand-lettered signs.

Jerri's Cherry Pie

Pies and desserts are always the grand finale to dinner on the ground. There's a couple of cherry pie recipes in our family. This is a recent addition from Jerri Pruitt, a caterer in Franklin who often provides the food when Wy, Ash, or I are working at home and can't cook for the TV or photo-shoot crews.

MAKES **8** SERVINGS

PIE CRUST

2 cups all-purpose flour
½ teaspoon salt
⅔ cup solid vegetable shortening, chilled
6 to 7 tablespoons ice water

PIE FILLING

2 cans (16 ounces each) cherries packed in water
¾ cup sugar
¼ cup cornstarch
1 tablespoon butter
Red food coloring

1. *Make the crust:* In a large bowl, combine the flour and salt. With a pastry blender, 2 knives held like scissors, or your fingertips, cut shortening into flour mixture until the mixture resembles small peas. Gradually drizzle in the water, tossing with a fork, until the dough comes together and cleans the side of the bowl; don't add too much water, since the dough should not be too sticky. Divide the dough into two-thirds and one-third portions. Flatten each into a disk, wrap in plastic wrap, and chill in the refrigerator for at least 1 hour.

2. On a floured surface, roll the larger piece of dough into a 13-inch circle, about ⅛ inch thick. Fit into a 9-inch pie plate and trim off any excess overhang. Combine the smaller piece of dough with the trimmings, and on a floured surface, roll out to a 9-inch circle. Using a knife or a fluted pastry-wheel cutter, cut the dough into ¾-inch-wide strips.

3. Preheat the oven to 350°.

4. *Make the filling:* Drain 1 cup of liquid from the cherries and pour into a saucepan. Stir in the sugar and the cornstarch. Add the butter. Place over medium heat and bring to a boil. Then cook, stirring, until thickened, 1 minute. Remove from the heat and stir in the cherries and enough food coloring for desired color. Pour the filling into the crust. Weave the strips of dough over the top of the pie in a lattice pattern. Pinch the ends of the strips to the edge of the pie. Place on a baking sheet.

5. Bake in the 350° oven until the crust is golden brown and the filling is bubbly, about 60 minutes. If the crust browns too quickly toward the end, cover loosely with aluminum foil. Remove to a wire rack. Serve warm or chilled.

Are you hungry for a simpler, more satisfying way of life? Begin visualizing it.

*What a choice: If you could
have five years of free service
from only one of the following,
whom would you pick—cook,
chauffeur, masseuse, house
cleaner, or personal assistant?*

Polly's Deviled Eggs

My Mom's eggs are legendary! We call them Church Eggs, and they are always a hit for family reunions or community get-togethers. In the early '80s, my Mom cooked on towboats along the Ohio River, and these were one of the crews' favorites from her galley. It was on one of those riverboats that she met the captain, Wib Rideout. He enjoyed her cooking so much, he married her.

MAKES 24 DEVILED EGGS

- **1 dozen large eggs**
- **⅔ cup mayonnaise-style salad dressing or mayonnaise (regular, reduced-fat, or nonfat)**
- **2 tablespoons prepared yellow mustard**
- **½ cup sweet pickle relish, squeezed of excess liquid**
- **2 teaspoons Worcestershire sauce**
- **6 drops hot-pepper sauce, or more or less to taste**
- **½ teaspoon salt**
- **¼ to ½ teaspoon white pepper**
- **Paprika, for garnish**

1. Place eggs in large saucepan. Cover with cold water. Bring slowly to just under a boil. Then gently cook for 10 minutes.

2. Carefully pour off the hot water and cover the eggs with ice water. Let stand for 15 minutes.

3. Gently crack the eggs and peel under cold running water, starting from the large end. (There should be an air pocket under the large end, making the peeling easy to start from this point.)

4. Cut the eggs in half lengthwise with a long thin knife. Remove the yolks and place in a medium bowl. Set the whites aside. Mash the yolks with a fork. Mix in the remaining ingredients (except paprika) until they have the consistency of mashed potatoes. If the filling is too thick, add a little more pickle juice or salad dressing, depending on your own preference. Spoon the filling into the hollowed-out whites. Sprinkle with paprika. Serve or cover and refrigerate for up to 1 day.

Sunday after service at Mark's, enjoying dinner in Fellowship Hall

Choices: Mayonnaise or Miracle Whip?

I urge you to question everything about your life. Once you begin to examine your beliefs and actions, you will gain awareness. Not surprisingly, once you become aware, you'll see you have choices. Choices are sacred. Whenever you feel trapped, know that your mind can always free you. Choices are the keys to opening the prison door in your mind. If you feel like things are out of your control, realize you can still get to be in control of your reactions to them. Control is an illusion anyway. Security is just a superstition. The only real security comes from within and from knowing that when you can't change the way things are around you, you can still change the way you feel inside about them.

Where you are in your life right this minute is a result of all the choices you've ever made. If you truly want to find happiness by transforming your life into what you dream it could be, you must first take responsibility for where you are and how you got there. If you accept this, you'll be free to change and move forward. If not, you'll continue to be unhappy and see yourself as the victim. There's freedom and peace, or misery and fear.

You get to choose.

These are my reasons to cook:

love,

nutrition,

Tradition,

and

celebration

- **A Mother's Love**   **Single-Mom Food**
- **From One Generation to Another**

We live in a transient society. Our family members often live in other states, and even if some of them live in the same town we do, our lives are so hectic we may not see each other much.

Our culture is instant, technological, materialistic, and disposable—an unappealing description, but unfortunately very true. That's why today tradition and rituals are more important than ever. These are the threads that intertwine our early lives with those we love, and continue to weave us into the community, strengthening the bonds of our society. We are like individual pieces of cloth, and tradition and rituals sew us tightly together to make a beautiful quilt called family. The family ties of home provide all of us our identity and help us define ourselves from within instead of by the constantly changing culture around us. When we feel accepted by our family members, our self-confidence makes us long to be part of something larger than ourselves.

Because of the incessant intrusion of the media, we live in houses without walls. Impressionable children are bombarded by the popular culture more than has ever happened in history. They know and care more about celebrities than about their own relatives or neighbors. They feel a relationship with their idols, more so than with their loved ones. And these stars don't know or care about them. Some celebrities are irresponsible and make terrible role models.

There's no more obvious place to weave family members together than the kitchen table—no better way to hand down tradition and carry on rituals, whether

When you say, "Pass the salt," you're really passing around your family history and preserving your personal culture.

Thanksgiving at Mom's (from left): That's my sister-in-law Middy, brother Mark, Nana, Wib, and Wynonna.

it's saying grace, celebrating a birthday, communicating about day-to-day life, or telling family stories.

Open Mouth, Insert Salty Foot

Recently I was having lunch with award-winning film director Ron Howard (*Apollo 13* and *Ransom*) and trying to act nonchalant. Since "The Andy Griffith Show" was my favorite TV show, I was experiencing major flashbacks of him as Opie in scenes with Andy, Aunt Bea, and Barney. During a pause in the conversation, I looked over at him and said, "Please pass the salt, Opie."

A MOTHER'S LOVE

Mom's joy was her family, and that was more than enough.

Mama only allowed herself two luxuries during the time we were growing up. The first was Jergens hand lotion in a white bottle with a black label sitting next to the kitchen sink. We didn't have a dishwasher, and we were a family of six. When it got near the dinner hour, she would take off her simple Bulova watch and put it next to the Jergens. I would sit at the kitchen table doing my homework and watch her put together a meal for six hungry people. Afterward, she'd clear the table, wash the dishes, straighten up the kitchen, and let out a sigh. She would reach for the Jergens and rub the lotion slowly into her tired hands.

The other luxury in Mom's life? There were two rosebushes out in our backyard. When they were blooming, she would cut a few blossoms and arrange them in a clear drinking glass on the kitchen table. Daddy gave away glasses for every gasoline fill-up at his station, so we always had plenty.

My Daddy passed away, but my Mama still lives in that same house I was raised in. It's a big, three-story frame house with an attic and a front porch. She moved it around the block to another location when the hospital in our town expanded and took over our old neighborhood. That house is like a member of the family. Mama even dug up the rosebushes and moved them, too.

"Trees are sanctuaries. Whoever knows how to speak to them, whoever knows how to listen to them, can learn truth."

—HERMANN HESSE

The only thing that remained from the old neighborhood was the family tree. I don't mean the kind of tree that charts your lineage. I'm talking about a magnificent oak that stood guard where our front gate had once been. It watched over us since before I was born, when Ogden and Sallie Ellen, my Judd grandparents, lived there.

"Tree," as I imaginatively called it, watched everyone who came and went in our lives. Some of my happiest days in life were spent playing in its sheltering shade. Every time I'd visit Mom for the last decade, I'd go back to the parking lot where our house had been and embrace lonely Tree.

A few weeks ago, while Wy and Ashley were in Ashland, they went to visit Tree and came upon a terrible discovery. Construction workers were preparing to cut it down! My girls had the cut-up tree brought to me in Peaceful Valley. Wy thinks we should use Tree's wood to make all of us rocking chairs for the front porch. Ashley suggests we turn it into a rose arbor in the backyard. I believe Tree would make a very special meditation chapel deep in my woods. It will be nice to have Tree over my head sheltering me again.

Mom with Tree moments before it was cut down

Waldorf Salad

Food as reward. Mom made this for special occasions—if someone got a great report card, a good-citizenship certificate, or had a piano recital. The original came from the Waldorf-Astoria Hotel in New York City.

MAKES 8 SERVINGS

DRESSING

½ cup mayonnaise

½ of 8-ounce container frozen
    nondairy whipped topping, thawed

SALAD

4 Granny Smith or Delicious apples,
    cored, cut into bite-size pieces, and
    sprinkled with a little fresh lemon
    juice to prevent darkening

½ cup raisins

½ cup diced celery

½ cup chopped walnuts

Lettuce leaves, for making a bed for
    serving

Sprinkling of cinnamon, for garnish

1. *Make the dressing:* In a small bowl, combine mayonnaise and whipped topping.

2. *Make the salad:* In a large bowl, mix apples, raisins, celery, and walnuts. Fold in dressing. Refrigerate until well chilled. Serve on lettuce. You may sprinkle the top with a little cinnamon.

Easy Onionettes

The top ten anti-aging veggies and fruits (in alphabetical order) are: avocado, berries, broccoli, cabbage, carrots, citrus fruits, grapes, onions, spinach, and tomatoes.

MAKES 16 SMALL OPEN-FACE SANDWICHES (THESE CAN BE CUT EVEN SMALLER FOR BITE-SIZE)

¼ **cup grated Parmesan cheese**
¼ **cup mayonnaise or mayonnaise-style creamy salad dressing, regular, reduced-fat, or nonfat**
4 **slices good-quality wheat bread, crusts removed**
16 **very thin slices Vidalia or other sweet onion**

1. Preheat the broiler.

2. In a small bowl, mix together the cheese and mayonnaise. Spread evenly on the bread slices. Cut each into 4 equal squares. Place an onion slice on each square.

3. Broil 4 to 5 inches from the heat until browned, about 2 minutes. Serve immediately.

Everybody Has a Story to Tell

The master Southern storyteller Pat Conroy, in his autobiographical novels *The Prince of Tides* and *The Great Santini,* captures the complex universal themes of family relationships.

When I was writing my life story, *Love Can Build a Bridge,* Pat and I had a deep conversation about how important it is to keep family stories alive. Pat also agrees that the kitchen table is a great place to do it! Tonight, share with your kids how you and your husband and their grandparents met. Ask them what their childhood memories are.

Healthy habits are learned in the same way as unhealthy ones—practice. What are your habits and routines? I try to get plenty of exercise, but it isn't always possible with my busy sleeping schedule.

Vegomatically

We juice at our house and find that it's a fast and healthy way to get plenty of fruit as well as veggies, such as carrots and celery, into our diet.

Once I drank carrot juice with my sausage and gravy. It's like combining stripes with plaids.

Sausages with Milk Gravy

From the mouth of Julia Child: "I'd rather eat a small portion of something good than a big portion of anything called 'health food.'" From the perfectly lined lips of Naomi Judd: "All things in moderation." Although most days for breakfast I have fresh carrot juice, fruit, plain yogurt with banana, raisins, and walnuts mixed in, and whole-wheat toast—so-called health food—once in a while, I hanker for my childhood starter of sausage and gravy. Tennessee Ernie Ford told me once when we were eating together after a country fair in Washington State, "When I was growing up, we put gravy on everything but our shoes."

MAKES 4 SERVINGS

1 pound breakfast sausage patties

GRAVY
3½ tablespoons all-purpose flour
¼ teaspoon dried marjoram
1 to 2 tablespoons butter or margarine, if needed
2 cups milk
½ teaspoon salt
⅛ teaspoon black pepper

1. Heat a large, heavy skillet (I love cast iron) over medium heat. Add the patties and cook until browned and cooked through, about 6 minutes per side. Remove the patties with a slotted spatula to paper towels to drain.

2. *Make the gravy:* Reduce the heat to medium-low. Into the pan drippings, slowly stir the flour and marjoram to make a thick paste. (If the sausages are lean and there's not a lot of pan drippings, add the butter to the skillet and melt.) Gradually whisk in the milk and cook, whisking frequently, until gravy is thick and bubbly, 2 to 3 minutes. Add the salt and pepper. Crumble 1 or 2 of the cooked sausages into the gravy, if you like.

3. Serve the sausages with eggs and biscuits, and spoon the gravy over them. (If I'm rushing out the door, I'll put a sausage in the middle of a biscuit to eat in the car.) Gobble and go.

Potato Salad

Mom's potato salad—where do I start! No one can make potato salad like hers. People have studied it, almost microscopically. Her secret? Pssst . . . c'mere and I'll tell you: She lets the warm, cooked potatoes sit in bottled French dressing before mixing them with all the other ingredients.

MAKES 6 TO 8 SERVINGS

- **4 Idaho baking potatoes (about 5 inches long, about 1¼ pounds), with skins**
- **1 teaspoon salt**
- **½ cup bottled French dressing**
- **3 large eggs**
- **1 cup diced celery**
- **1 cup diced sweet onion**
- **¾ cup sweet pickle relish**
- **1½ cups mayonnaise or mayonnaise-style creamy salad dressing**
- **2 tablespoons prepared mustard**

1. Cover potatoes in a large saucepan with water. Bring to boiling and cook until fork-tender, about 30 minutes. Drain. When cool enough to handle but still very warm, peel the potatoes and then cube. Place the warm potatoes in a large bowl. Add the salt and

French dressing, tossing to coat. (You can even let the potatoes sit in the refrigerator overnight at this point.)

2. Meanwhile, place the eggs in a medium saucepan. Cover with cold water. Bring to just under a boil and simmer for 10 minutes. Drain and return the eggs to the pot, covering with ice water. Let stand 15 minutes. Peel the eggs under cold running water, beginning with the large end. Cut into small cubes and reserve.

3. To the potatoes, add the celery, onion, and pickle relish.

4. In a small bowl, stir together the mayonnaise and mustard. With a spatula, fold the mayonnaise mixture into the potato mixture until thoroughly blended. Add the egg and gently stir just to evenly distribute. This is one of those dishes that is even better the next day.

Dorthey—our housekeeper and one of my best friends—and me trying to duplicate Mom's potato salad

Then and Now

When I was little, Tuesday was my favorite day because that's when the *Saturday Evening Post* arrived. I would rush home after school and go straight to the refrigerator to the green plastic bowl on the second shelf where Mom kept her potato salad. I'd dish up a big helping, grab a Pepsi, a bag of Fritos, the *Saturday Evening Post,* and sit myself down in front of the TV and turn on Soupy Sales. Later I graduated to "American Bandstand." It didn't get any better than that!

I've long since given up soft drinks for water, natural fruit juices, and herbal ice teas. A good fruit drink is cranberry juice, since it helps prevent bacteria from anchoring to bladder walls. The key is to drink real cranberry juice and not those sweetened ones. It's going to be tarter than you're used to—it'll make you pucker—but the tarter it is, the better it works. Drink 16 ounces of fresh cranberry juice a day to flush out bacteria that cause urinary-tract infections. I mix it with fresh apple juice for a great taste.

Believe it or not, the average American (who *is* this person?) consumes the equivalent of forty-five teaspoons of sugar a day. The recommended limit is only twelve.

When I'm with Grace and Elijah, all my cares disappear.

Here's a little rhyme about finishing what you start:
If a task is once begun,
Never leave it 'til it's done.
Be the labor great or small,
Do it well or not at all.

Reading Is to the Mind What Exercise Is to the Body

Children benefit greatly from structure and rituals. A family ritual everyone can enjoy is reading to children at bedtime. My grandkids Elijah and Grace make me do all the characters' voices. Just ask former First Lady Barbara Bush about how important reading is. She's absolutely passionate about making sure children and adults learn to read. She also has a great sense of humor—she once said something so funny she made me spit Perrier water out my nose while we were eating lunch together. Ouch!

They say conscience is that small inner voice . . . but sometimes mine screams pretty loudly. My Mama gave me my conscience, and Daddy taught me his work ethic. Wy, Ashley, and I now call it Personal Excellence. It's the Judd way.

Scalloped Cheesy Potatoes

Let's all say "cheesy" together! This dish is practically in the same category as macaroni and cheese! According to a 1997 poll, Wisconsin (the cheese state), Michigan, West Virginia, Mississippi, and Alabama have the most overweight citizens. Hey, I only report the news! I love cheese, too, but if the girdle fits, wear it!

MAKES 8 SERVINGS

1 can (10¾ ounces) condensed
   cream of chicken soup, undiluted
2 cups (8 ounces) shredded Cheddar
   cheese
About 2 pounds russet potatoes,
   peeled and sliced thin
1 medium onion, sliced thin
¾ cup Ritz cracker crumbs
   (about 18 crackers)

1. Preheat the oven to 425°. Grease a 13 × 9 × 2-inch baking dish.

2. In a large bowl, stir together the soup and cheese. With a rubber spatula, fold in the potatoes and onion until thoroughly coated. Scrape into the prepared baking dish. Cover with aluminum foil.

3. Bake in the 425° oven until the potatoes are very tender, about 40 minutes. Remove the foil. Sprinkle the top with the cracker crumbs. Bake until the top is golden brown, another 5 to 10 minutes. Let stand for 10 minutes before serving.

Broccoli-Cheese Casserole

Rich, warm, and satisfying as a mother's love.

MAKES 8 SERVINGS

¾ **stick or 6 tablespoons butter or**
   margarine
2 **tablespoons all-purpose flour**
1 **can (10¾ ounces) condensed cream**
   of mushroom soup, undiluted
1 **cup shredded Cheddar cheese, mild**
   or sharp, to your taste
2 **bags (1 pound each) frozen broccoli**
   cuts, cooked according to package
   directions and drained, or 2 pounds
   fresh broccoli, lightly steamed
3 **large eggs, well beaten**

TOPPING

1 **tablespoon butter or margarine**
1 **cup fresh soft bread crumbs**
   (2 to 3 slices bread)

1. Preheat oven to 350°. Grease a 2-quart
   casserole.

2. In a large skillet, melt the butter over
   medium heat. Stir in the flour until
   well blended. Then stir in the soup.
   Cook, stirring, until thickened,
   30 seconds to 1 minute. Stir in cheese
   until smooth. Remove the skillet from

the heat. Stir in the broccoli and eggs.
Spoon into the prepared casserole dish.

3. *Make the topping:* In a small saucepan,
   melt the butter. Add the crumbs and
   toss to mix. Sprinkle over the casserole.

4. Bake in the 350° oven, uncovered,
   until the filling is bubbly and the topping is lightly golden and crusty, about
   30 minutes. Let stand for 10 minutes
   before serving.

Fresh Green Beans and Potatoes

When we didn't want meat, Mama made a summer meal of these green beans and potatoes, with sliced tomatoes, fresh corn on the cob, and a pan of cornbread. If you want to omit the bacon, use a little soy sauce or dillweed for flavoring instead.

MAKES 8 SERVINGS

8 slices bacon, cut into ½-inch pieces
4 pounds green beans, trimmed and snapped or cut into bite-size pieces
2 big onions (optional), cut into quarters
Water as needed, about 3 cups
10 to 12 small new red potatoes, scrubbed and with skins, halved
½ teaspoon salt
¼ teaspoon black pepper

1. In a large pot, cook the bacon to render the fat, and then remove the bacon to paper towels to drain. Or, if you have bacon fat that you've saved, heat a ½ cup until sizzling. Or use ¼ cup bacon fat and ¼ cup vegetable oil.

2. Stir in the green beans and the onions, if using, and cook until beans have absorbed some of the fat and turned bright green. Then add enough water to come to within 1 inch of top of beans. Cover and cook over low heat until almost done, about 1 hour.

3. Add the potatoes, salt, pepper, and more water if necessary. Cook until the potatoes are done, about 15 minutes. If you want, you can scatter the bacon pieces over the top to serve.

Wilted Salad

Mom was always on the lookout for new recipes to spring on her family. This one has bacon fat, so she knew we'd go for it. Some call this "killed salad." Hey, don't ask me—I just wrote the book.

MAKES 4 SERVINGS

- **6 thick-cut slices bacon (about 8 ounces)**
- **½ head leaf lettuce, washed, dried, and torn into bite-size pieces**
- **4 green onions, cut into ¼-inch pieces**
- **¼ cup cider vinegar or balsamic vinegar**
- **¼ teaspoon black pepper**

1. In a large skillet, cook the bacon over medium heat until crisp. Remove the bacon and keep the fat warm over low heat. Drain the bacon on paper towels, and then crumble it into bite-size pieces.

2. In a large bowl, combine the leaf lettuce, bacon, and onion.

3. Add the vinegar to the bacon fat. Pour the warm mixture over the lettuce mixture and add the pepper, tossing to mix. Serve immediately.

SINGLE-MOM FOOD

Life as I had known it ended at seventeen, when I became unexpectedly pregnant with Wynonna. From the first moment I realized she was there, I loved that unborn baby. She was a human life, not a "choice." Did you know that 113 out of every thousand teenage girls get pregnant and are unwed? That adds up to a million a year. They're spittin' 'em out like a popcorn machine! At dinner tonight, ask what everyone thinks is causing this, besides the obvious.

I remember one afternoon in 1964 my first mother-in-law, Billie, was going to teach me how to make real Southern ice tea. She brought out her favorite antique leaded-glass pitcher. I poured the hot tea into it! Remember I'm only a senior in high school then and dumb as a box of hair. Of course it broke, and hot tea ran all over the counter and all down the sides of the cabinets. Billie, who was standing in a pool of tea, gently took my hand and quietly explained, "Next time, let's first put a big metal spoon in the pitcher before you pour in the hot tea, so the spoon can absorb all the heat." Now, thirty years later, every time I make ice tea, I think of that little tip of encouragement.

Been There, Done That, Got the T-Shirt

I have been a teenage mom, a divorced mom, a single working mom, a welfare mom, a college-student mom, a celebrity mom, a very sick mom, and a well mom. Having to support my kids alone, I've worked as a waitress, model, clerk, secretary, and R.N., among other things. About the only job I haven't done is being a mechanic. Traditionally speaking, I was out of order. I didn't fall into the usual pattern.

Twenty-five years ago, I was a struggling single mom living in a funky house off Sunset Boulevard in Hollywood, California. I became friends with Nancy Balazs, who lived across the street and was in the same boat, raising her daughter Gabrielle. Since I didn't even have a car, every Friday when we got our paychecks, Nancy would take me, along with all the kids, to the grocery store. On one of these trips, Nancy shared with me her recipe for this great chicken-and-rice dish she called Chicken Continental—a fancy name for something extremely easy to make. It's rich and creamy and very satisfying. All you need to go with it is a vegetable and a salad. This makes a wonderful dish for company, especially if your friends and family are cutting back on the amount of beef they eat. In recent years, instead of the usual white rice, I've been using an aromatic yellow rice for its slightly nutty flavor and warm yellow color. Gabrielle, who is still best friends with Ashley, now makes Chicken Continental for her family, so the tradition continues.

Today, seven out of ten women with kids under eighteen work outside the home as well as doing regular housework.

Chicken Continental

MAKES **6** SERVINGS

½ **stick or** ¼ **cup unsalted butter**

6 **boneless, skinned chicken breast halves (about 5 ounces each)**

3 **cans (10¾ ounces each) condensed cream of chicken soup, undiluted**

3 **level tablespoons dried celery flakes**

2 **teaspoons dried thyme**

2 **cups raw Indian rice (Mahatma) with saffron flavoring or 1 package (16 ounces) yellow rice, cooked according to package directions**

1. Preheat the oven to 350°.

2. In a large skillet, melt the butter over medium heat. Add the chicken and brown on both sides, about 6 minutes. Remove the chicken and set aside.

3. Into the drippings in the skillet, whisk the soup, celery flakes, and thyme until well blended. Heat until bubbly. Stir in the rice. Spoon the mixture into a 13 × 9 × 2-inch baking dish. Place the chicken breasts on top and push them down into the rice mixture until almost covered. Cover the dish with aluminum foil.

4. Bake in the 350° oven until the chicken breasts are no longer pink in the center, about 30 minutes. Remove the foil and bake for another 10 minutes. Let stand for 10 minutes before serving.

Lower the Mud in Your Blood

Beans are good for the heart. The more beans you eat, the lower your cholesterol is. Fifty-two percent of Americans have cholesterol above two hundred. The norm should be less than two hundred. With cornbread, beans make a good substitute for meat and potatoes. The complementary proteins in beans and corn (which is a grain) make a complete protein. At one time, Wy, Ashley, and I were all vegetarians. Now only Ashley remains devoted. But Wy and I are still vegetarians in between meals, and we've cut down on red meat considerably.

When I make plain cornbread, I spoon molasses over it. I don't buy molasses or honey in a store, 'cause I prefer to get it from local farmers. I want to support local merchants, plus it helps decrease spring allergies since pollen is in it!

Baked Beans with Franks

Baked beans and franks go together like Tarzan and Jane, Sonny and Cher. This is not just a picnic dish, or an easy Saturday-night meal. This was a staple in my house when I was a single mom.

MAKES 6 TO 8 SERVINGS

12 slices bacon
1 large onion, diced
2 cans (28 ounces each) pork and beans
¾ cup packed brown sugar
¼ cup Worcestershire sauce
2 tablespoons prepared yellow mustard
2 hot dogs, sliced (we use turkey wieners)

1. Preheat the oven to 375°.

2. In a large skillet, cook the bacon over low heat until crisp, 4 to 6 minutes. Remove the bacon to paper towels to drain, and then crumble.

3. To the hot bacon fat, add the onion and cook, stirring, until softened, about 4 minutes.

4. In a large bowl, combine the crumbled bacon, the onion along with the bacon fat, and the pork and beans. Stir in the sugar, Worcestershire sauce, and mustard. Scrape into a 13 × 9 × 2-inch baking dish and place the dish on a baking sheet. Cover with aluminum foil.

5. Bake in the 375° oven for 30 minutes. Remove the foil from the dish and place the sliced hot dogs on top of the baked beans. Bake, uncovered, until the hot dogs are heated through, another 10 minutes. This is better if browned slightly on top.

Mexican Cornbread

This is real good for real folks who are real hungry.

MAKES 8 SERVINGS

¼ cup vegetable oil
2 cups self-rising flour*
½ cup white cornmeal
1 large egg
1 can (11 ounces) mexi-corn, undrained
1 cup shredded Cheddar cheese
¾ cup milk, or more as needed

1. Preheat the oven to 425°. Into a large cast-iron skillet, pour the oil. Heat in oven until oil is hot but not smoking.

2. Meanwhile, in a large bowl, mix the flour, cornmeal, egg, corn, cheese, and milk. If the mixture is too stiff, thin with a little more milk, although the batter should be somewhat stiff, and not too thin.

3. Carefully remove the hot skillet from the oven. Scrape the batter into the skillet and spread evenly.

4. Bake in the 425° oven until golden brown, about 20 to 25 minutes. Remove the skillet to a wire rack to cool for 10 minutes. Cut the cornbread into wedges and serve warm.

*FLOUR POWER TIP
You can substitute regular all-purpose flour for the self-rising flour. Use 2 cups of regular all-purpose flour and mix in 1 tablespoon baking powder. Then make the recipe exactly as above.

Shell Macaroni and Tuna Salad

This makes a good filling for stuffed tomatoes. Somebody told me back in the '70s when I was an "Earth Mother" that mayo was a good hair-conditioner. Not only did it make my hair look greasy, but flies buzzed around my head.

MAKES 6 SERVINGS

- **4 cups cooked medium shell macaroni (about 2 cups uncooked)**
- **2 cans (6 ounces each) tuna, drained and flaked**
- **½ cup chopped celery**
- **3 tablespoons finely chopped onion**
- **1 teaspoon grated lemon rind**
- **1 tablespoon fresh lemon juice**
- **½ teaspoon black pepper**
- **¼ teaspoon salt**
- **½ cup mayonnaise**
- **Lettuce leaves, for serving**

1. In a medium bowl, combine the macaroni, tuna, celery, and onion.

2. In a small bowl, stir together the lemon rind, lemon juice, pepper, salt, and mayonnaise. Fold the mayonnaise mixture into the macaroni mixture. Serve on a bed of lettuce. You can refrigerate this salad for up to 3 days.

"Depends" on Who Said . . .

What's this I hear about June Allyson going back to cloth diapers? . . . When Wynonna was about a year old and we were living in a $75-a-month apartment, I used cloth diapers. I washed them in the bathtub since we had no washer or dryer. Once in a while I'd save up enough deposits from pop bottles to go to the Wishy Washy Laundromat. Later we got a used Maytag wringer washer. Wy was always threatening to put Ashley through the wringer and make her "flat as a pancake."

When they were teenagers and I was working as an R.N., Wy, Ashley, and I finally got an electric washer and dryer. They excitedly brought their friends off the school bus to see it. Their friends just stared at it blankly, saying, "So?" They didn't understand my love affair with a major appliance.

The Queen Will Serve You Now

I always dress for comfort in the kitchen—a washable outfit, no apron, house slippers, and my rhinestone tiara. You think I'm kidding? The tiara serves as a hairnet.

We used our Maytag wringer washer, then hung our clothes to dry in the sunshine and fresh air.

Polly's Potato Pancakes

Say this recipe name three times real fast, but DO NOT ever say "pancake" in front of Ashley. Use leftover mashed potatoes for these crispy potato cakes.

MAKES 12 CAKES

- **2 heaping cups mashed potatoes**
- **1 large egg, well beaten**
- **⅓ cup chopped leeks, onion, or scallions**
- **⅓ cup all-purpose flour**
- **½ teaspoon salt**
- **¼ teaspoon black pepper**
- **¼ cup vegetable oil or bacon fat, for frying**

1. Place the mashed potatoes in a bowl and make a well in the center. Add the egg, leeks, flour, salt, and pepper and stir until well mixed.

2. In a large skillet, heat the oil over medium-high heat.

3. Using a greased soup spoon, carefully drop heaping spoonfuls of the potato mixture into the hot oil, about 6 at a time; avoid crowding. Fry until edges are browned, about 3 minutes. Turn over with a metal spatula. Fry 3 minutes or until golden. Remove with the spatula to paper towels to drain.

Cornmeal Mush

Multiple-choice question for definition of mush:
(1) what you say to sled dogs
(2) something soggy and boggy
(3) when lovebirds are overly romantic
(4) a warm, alternative carbohydrate side dish.

MAKES 6 SERVINGS

3½ cups water
1 cup white cornmeal
1 cup cold water
1 teaspoon salt
About 8 teaspoons vegetable oil or bacon fat, for frying
Butter and maple syrup, for serving

1. In a 3-quart heavy saucepan, bring the 3½ cups of water to a boil. Meanwhile, grease an 8 × 8 × 2-inch square baking dish.

2. In a medium bowl, stir together the cornmeal, cold water, and salt. Very gradually whisk the cornmeal mixture into the boiling water, whisking constantly to avoid any lumping. When the mixture returns to the boil, reduce the heat to a simmer. Cover the saucepan and simmer, whisking every 5 minutes, until thickened, about 25 minutes.

3. Pour the mixture into the prepared baking dish. Refrigerate until firm enough to slice, about 4 hours.

4. Onto a cutting board, unmold the cornmeal mixture. Cut into slices about ⅓ inch wide. (You should have 24 slices, 4 slices per serving.)★

5. In a large nonstick skillet, heat 2 teaspoons of the oil or bacon fat over medium-high heat. Working in batches and adding more oil or bacon fat as needed, add the slices of mush and cook until crisp and brown, about 10 minutes on the first side, and then 6 to 8 minutes on the second side. Transfer to paper towels to drain and then serve hot with butter and maple syrup.

★ TIP
When you unmold the mush from the baking dish, you can, for variety, cut it up in the following way: Cut the square into quarters, and then cut each quarter into 9 slices, for a total of 36 slices. Each serving is then 6 slices.

Home is the anchor of our existence, our little corner of peace, a resting place for the heart.

FROM ONE GENERATION TO ANOTHER

Recently Wy, Ashley, and I were having supper on the back deck—Ashley was reading Baudelaire, Wy, *People Magazine*—and I was insisting they stop reading at the table so we could carry on a conversation.

Wy looked up from her plate. "Mother, I'm thirty-three years old, and as long as I can remember, you've been telling sister and me to get in touch with our intuition. What is intuition?"

I directed my response to Ashley. "Well, Rousseau defines intuition as the divine intelligence which allows us to discern in the twinkling of an eye between that which is true and that which is vain and deceptive knowledge." Wynonna, who got it immediately, exclaimed, "Intuition is when your gut gets it before your brain gets around to figuring it out. Cool!"

I challenge you to get in touch with your inner knowing. Take off that role-playing mask others have talked you into wearing, and don't be afraid to become who you really are! Plus, you don't become successful by trying to be like someone else, but by finally becoming who you truly are.

John Wayne said, "Courage is being scared to death but saddling up anyhow."

Give a man a fish, and he eats for one day.

Teach a man to fish, and he eats for a lifetime.

Salmon Patties

My Mom made this practically every Friday night when I was growing up. I make it at home with lima beans for lunch.

MAKES 5 CAKES

> 2 cans (7½ ounces each) good-quality salmon or 1 large can (14¾ ounces), drained and flaked
> 1 cup crushed Saltine cracker crumbs (about 24 crackers)
> 1 large egg, lightly beaten
> ½ teaspoon salt
> ¼ teaspoon pepper
> ¼ to ½ cup vegetable oil
> Ketchup or cocktail sauce, for serving

1. In a medium bowl, mix together the salmon, cracker crumbs, egg, salt, and pepper, breaking up the salmon well. Shape the salmon mixture into five 3-inch patties, using about ½ cup of mixture for each—make sure they are firm.

2. In a large, heavy skillet, heat the oil over medium-high heat. Place the patties in the skillet, making sure they don't touch. Cook until browned on both sides, about 5 minutes total. Serve hot with ketchup on the side.

Guess Who's Coming to Dinner

My playmates always wanted to come to my house for meals 'cause Mom was such a good cook and being at our house was fun. I never know who my girls will be bringing home with them. When Hollywood heartthrob Matthew McConaughey was shooting the movie *A Time to Kill* with Ashley, she brought him home to meet us. We didn't do much but a lot of nothing, relaxing outdoors. Matthew stayed up in the barn. Through my kitchen window, I'd watch him saunter down to the house, looking like a matinee idol farmhand (visions of Paul Newman in *Hud*). After he polished off an entire pan of meatloaf made from my mother's recipe, Matthew pushed back from the table and drawled, "Much obliged, Ma'am. I reckon I best be gettin' back out yonder to finish mendin' them fences and lookin' for them stray dogies, now."

Mowing for Meatloaf

There's one in every family. One of the essentials for any well-fed family is a good meatloaf recipe. When my Mom cooked on a riverboat, once the crew had tasted her version, it became a standard. Steve Hemplepp, a friend of my brother Mark, would cut Mom's yard in exchange for a piece of this meatloaf. Neighbor ladies paid her in chickens for birthing their babies, and . . . But seriously now, next time you drive by Mom's house, check out who's behind that push-mower. It could be the singer Meatloaf himself. (Slices of this meatloaf cold make wonderful sandwiches.)

MAKES 10 SERVINGS

2⅓ cups coarsely crushed soda crackers (1½ tubes from package)
2 pounds lean ground beef
½ pound breakfast sausage patties
1 large egg
2 medium onions, chopped
1 medium green bell pepper, minced
¾ cup ketchup + ¼ cup for the top
⅓ cup Worcestershire sauce
1 teaspoon salt
½ teaspoon black pepper

1. Preheat the oven to 325°. In a heavy-duty, plastic food-storage bag, place the crackers, seal, and roll over with a rolling pin until crushed but not powdery.

2. Take any rings off your fingers and send them to me! In a large bowl, with clean hands, mix together all the ingredients except the ¼ cup ketchup for the top. Mix thoroughly but lightly, being careful not to pack the meat too much. Place in a 13 × 9 × 2-inch baking pan and shape into a loaf. Cover with aluminum foil.

3. Bake in the 325° oven for 45 minutes. Remove the foil. Spread the top of the loaf with the ¼ cup ketchup. Bake, uncovered, another 60 minutes. Let stand for 10 minutes before slicing.

Barbecued Chicken with Sauce

I learned this dish from my Mom and passed it on to my kids. Mashed potatoes or Yeast Rolls (page 167) are a must for soaking up the gravy in this dish.

MAKES 4 SERVINGS

- ¾ cup all-purpose flour
- 1 whole chicken (about 3½ pounds), giblets and liver removed for other use, cut into 8 serving pieces
- 3 tablespoons vegetable oil
- 2 medium onions

SAUCE

- 1 cup water
- ½ cup ketchup
- 2 tablespoons cider vinegar
- 1½ tablespoons Worcestershire sauce
- 1 tablespoon sugar
- 1 teaspoon salt
- 1 teaspoon dry mustard
- ½ teaspoon chili powder

1. On a sheet of waxed paper, spread the flour and roll the chicken in the flour to coat. Shake off any excess flour. In a large, heavy skillet, heat the oil. Working in two batches, cook the chicken until browned on all sides, about 7 minutes per batch, removing the chicken to a plate when browned.

2. Preheat the oven to 325°. Slice the onions and reserve.

3. *Make the sauce:* In a small bowl, stir together the water, ketchup, vinegar, Worcestershire sauce, sugar, salt, dry mustard, and chili powder.

4. In a 4-quart Dutch oven or deep oven-proof casserole with lid, place half of the chicken pieces in a single layer. Cover with half of the onions and half of the sauce. Repeat the layering. Cover the casserole.

5. Bake in the 325° oven for 2 hours, uncovering for the last 30 minutes for the chicken to brown on top. With tongs or a slotted spoon, remove the chicken pieces and onions to a platter and cover with aluminum foil to keep warm. Skim the fat from the sauce and discard. Spoon some of the sauce over the chicken and serve the rest in a sauceboat.

Today's women are looking for a simpler, more natural life-style. That's why home cooking is back by popular demand!

Green Beans with Bacon

This is probably the oldest recipe in our family. This dish can be halved or quartered.

MAKES **16** SERVINGS

½ **cup canola or other vegetable oil**
4 **pounds green beans, trimmed, strings removed and beans snapped or cut into bite-size pieces**
Water, as needed
½ **pound slab smoked bacon, cut into small chunks (1 × ½ × ¼ inch)**
1 **teaspoon salt**
½ **teaspoon black pepper**

1. In a large saucepan, heat the canola oil. Add the green beans and stir until coated with the oil. Add enough water to the saucepan to come to a depth of 1 inch. Stir the bacon, salt, and pepper into the beans. Bring to a boil over high heat.

2. Cover the saucepan and reduce the heat to medium. Cook until the beans are tender, stirring a few times, about 30 minutes. Transfer to a large serving bowl and serve.

Green Bean Casserole

Remember there's soups with half the fat, as well as reduced-sodium. Gee, if we had all this low-fat stuff around twenty years ago, Elvis might still be with us.

MAKES **6** SERVINGS

1 **can (10¾ ounces) condensed cream of mushroom soup, undiluted**
⅓ **cup milk**
1 **can (7 ounces) sliced mushrooms, drained**
2 **cans (14½ ounces each) French-style green beans, thawed and drained, or 4 cups cut fresh green beans, boiled until crisp-tender**
1 **can (8 ounces) sliced water chestnuts, drained**
2 **cans (2.8 ounces each) French-fried onions**
¾ **cup shredded Cheddar cheese, optional**

1. Preheat the oven to 350°.

2. In a 1½-quart casserole, stir together the soup, milk, and sliced mushrooms until combined. Stir in the green beans, water chestnuts, one can of the onions, and ½ cup of the cheese, if using. Cover with aluminum foil.

3. Bake in the 350° oven until the casserole is bubbly, about 45 minutes. Remove the foil from the casserole. Sprinkle the remaining can of onions on top of the casserole and the remaining ¼ cup of cheese, if using. Bake, uncovered, another 10 minutes. Let stand for 10 minutes before serving.

What were they thinking? Elijah and Grace are afraid of the "Jolly Green Giant"—
and does "Birds Eye" sound appealing to you guys?

Which would suit you best—a wildly turbulent life overflowing with adventure, joys and tragedies, intoxicating successes but stunning setbacks, or a happy and secure, safe, predictable life without such peaks and valleys?

Straight from the Earth to Your Plate

My Daddy's oldest sister, Aunt Pauline, was one of my favorite relatives. Throughout my childhood, I visited her often at her primitive farmhouse in Louisa, Kentucky. She'd holler at me to go out to the garden and pick her some "green 'maters." Since there was no running water, I'd wash them with well-drawn water and watch her fry them up on her woodstove. Talk about food bringing back wonderful memories!

If you haven't seen the movie *Fried Green Tomatoes*, rent it. It's all about tradition and food as an expression of love, as are *Babette's Feast* and *Like Water for Chocolate*. By the way, while you're at it, rent *Ruby in Paradise*, *Heat*, *A Time to Kill*, and *Kiss the Girls*, all featuring Ashley Judd. I'm a typical parent, so when I tell Ashley, like any proud mom, "I think it's great you know how to act in movies, but I'm much prouder that you know how to act in real life," she rolls her eyes back in her head and groans under her breath, "Oh, Muh-Thur!"

Coming Soon to a Table Near You . . . Fried Green Tomatoes

MAKES 4 SERVINGS

3 medium, firm green tomatoes (about 1 pound)

¼ teaspoon salt

¼ teaspoon black pepper

⅓ cup white cornmeal

About 2¼ cups solid vegetable shortening (1-pound can) or 2¼ cups bacon fat, for frying

Sugar, if needed, after frying (if added too soon, the tomatoes stick)

1. Cut each tomato into four ½-inch-thick slices. Season with the salt and pepper. On a sheet of waxed paper, spread the cornmeal. Dredge the slices of tomato in cornmeal, coating well on both sides.

2. In a large, heavy skillet, add enough shortening or bacon fat to come to a depth of ½ inch and heat over high heat until shimmering and starting to smoke a little. Add half of the tomato slices to the skillet. Lower the heat to medium-high. Cover the skillet and cook until the bottoms of the tomatoes are browned and the sizzling stops, about 4 minutes. Turn the tomatoes over with a slotted spatula. Cover and fry the second side, about 2 minutes. The tomatoes should be slightly soft around the firm edges. Remove the tomatoes with the spatula to paper towels to drain. Taste, and if too tart, sprinkle with sugar while still hot.

3. Repeat with the remaining tomato slices. Serve hot.

I'm just a kid living in an adult body.

A Real Career Highlight

I'd rather hang out with my kids than anybody. Recently, I went with Ashley, who's a basketball fanatic, to the last home basketball game of her alma mater's team, the famous University of Kentucky Wildcats. We talked our girlfriend singer Faith Hill into going with us and singing the National Anthem. Faith said okay, if we do something, too. So, before a crowd of 25,000 at halftime, Ashley and I darted out onto the gym floor as the cheerleaders spelled out the word "Kentucky." We lay down on the floor and created the last letter, "Y"! As we sprawled there, I leaned over and whispered to Ashley, "I'm glad we wore pants!"

When Ashley suggested she and I do a mother-daughter fun thing and spontaneously hop on a plane and fly to Chicago to see our Irish buddies U2 in concert, I said, "Sure, 'cause I'm a Rock 'n' Roll Mama!"

U2 and friends (from left): Edge, me, Bono (on top), Larry, and Ashley

Oh Bob, Bring Out Those Fa-a-a-bulous Prizes!

When the girls and I are appearing together at awards shows or major public events, we form our triangle, clasping our hands, and shout our special cheer: "Aka Paka, Piggly Wiggly, H G Hill, Who's Gonna Win? (insert the contestant's name) Will!" And off we go.

Wy and I used to visit with Make A Wish Fund kids on our bus after concerts. She would make trumpet sounds while announcing me: "Ladies and Gentlemen. Her Royal Majesty, the Queen of Everything!" On this cue, I'd burst through the door wearing my outrageous dress and rhinestone tiara, looking for all the world like a Fairy Godmother. Wy and I would have the excited children repeat these "magical" words after us: "Mekka Lekka Hi. Mikka Lekka Hiney Ho," and then fill in a rhyme appropriate to their medical condition. I'd touch them with my magic wand and grant their special wish.

Me as the "Queen of Everything." Hey, don't laugh—I bet you've got a weird fantasy, too.

We are the wealthiest nation on earth, but one in four children in America is hungry. This makes me hang my head in shame. If this bothers you, please send a donation to the Feed the Children Fund (1-800-627-4556). I know these good folks and have worked with them.

Wy and I fell in love with a little fan named Ashley, but my magic wand couldn't save her from cancer.

Hey Kids, Wanna Free Trip to the Moon?

To send your kids into outer space, try playing a psychiatrist on TV. When I actually portrayed one on a TV drama called "The Client," it was so scary a concept that Wy and Ashley wouldn't even watch. Just imagine your Mom as a shrink giving out advice to everybody! But Ashley did have to watch me playing a doctor once 'cause I was delivering her baby in her last episode of the series she started her acting career in, called "Sisters." Still, my favorite starring role is plain ol' Mom.

It's great for kids to see both parents in roles other than caretaker. They develop an awareness that we're also individuals—people who were once kids themselves but now simply live in bigger bodies.

Respect Your Mother Earth and Protect Our Planet

Something we can each do at home to help the world is recycling. Our kitchen has three garbage cans: one for glass, one for newspapers, and one for whatever. And there is a trash compactor for cans. My two-year-old grandson Elijah thinks this sorting out is fun. He looks at his garbage and figures out where it belongs, and then stands back and tosses it into the right place. I holler, "Slam dunk! One for the Jellybean!" This is an obvious opportunity to get your kids hip to respecting their other mother—Mother Earth—before their other Father—Time—runs out.

Applesauce Cake

There are two kinds of people in this world: those who like sweet stuff, such as chocolate, and those who like crunchy and salty. Which are you? My great-aunt Peg Burton passed this recipe down. It's my favorite cake because it's not too sweet and requires no icing.

MAKES 12 SERVINGS

- 1 cup raisins
- ¾ cup warm water
- 3⅓ cups all-purpose flour
- 2 cups sugar
- 2 tablespoons unsweetened cocoa powder
- 2 teaspoons baking powder
- 2 teaspoons baking soda
- 2 teaspoons ground cinnamon
- 1 teaspoon ground allspice
- ½ teaspoon ground cloves
- ½ teaspoon salt
- ⅔ cup butter, at room temperature
- 2 large eggs
- 2 cups sweetened applesauce
- 1 cup pecans or other nuts, chopped
- Whipped cream or vanilla ice cream, for serving (optional, but it's good!)

1. Preheat the oven to 350°. Grease the bottoms of two 8 × 8 × 2-inch square or 8-inch round layer cake pans. Line the bottoms of the pans with waxed paper and then grease the paper. In a small cup, soak the raisins in the warm water until softened, about 10 minutes. Drain the excess liquid.

2. Onto a clean sheet of waxed paper, sift together the flour, sugar, cocoa powder, baking powder, baking soda, cinnamon, allspice, cloves, and salt.

3. In a large bowl, with an electric mixer at low speed, beat together the butter, eggs, and applesauce until well blended. On low speed, beat in the flour mixture until well blended. Stir in the raisins and nuts. Scrape into the prepared pans, dividing equally.

4. Bake in the 350° oven until a wooden pick inserted in the center comes out clean, 45 to 50 minutes. Let the cakes cool completely in the pans on wire racks. Cut each cake into 6 pieces. Serve with a dollop of whipped cream or a scoop of vanilla ice cream, if you'd like.

Chocolate Meringue Pie

I remember watching Mom back in Ashland, Kentucky, teaching Ashley to make her famous chocolate meringue pie, just as she had shown me in that same kitchen 40 years ago, and I realized that Mom, through that simple act, was once again passing along her secrets of life, her recipes for living. Mom's strength of purpose, her devotion to family, her wacky sense of humor—all those traits that bind the Judd women together—it was all there as she chatted away, beating the meringue and spreading it over the top of

Ashley learned to bake as well as Mom. Well, almost.

the pie. Find a Judd woman in the kitchen and you're likely to find a chocolate meringue pie. We've also been known to have the leftovers for breakfast—really.

MAKES 8 SERVINGS

PIE CRUST

1½ **cups all-purpose flour**
2 **teaspoons sugar**
½ **teaspoon salt**
½ **cup solid vegetable shortening**
3 to 4 **tablespoons ice water**

CHOCOLATE FILLING

3 **large egg yolks**
1 **cup sugar**
6 **tablespoons all-purpose flour**
¼ **teaspoon salt**
3 **cups milk, scalded**
2 **squares (1 ounce each) unsweetened chocolate, chopped**
2 **tablespoons unsalted butter**
½ **teaspoon vanilla extract**

FOOLPROOF MERINGUE

1 **tablespoon cornstarch**
8 **tablespoons sugar**
⅓ **cup water**
Pinch salt
3 **large egg whites**

1. *Make the crust:* In a large bowl, stir together the flour, sugar, and salt. Cut in the shortening with a pastry blender or two knives used like a scissors, or mix with your fingertips until the mixture resembles coarse crumbs. Sprinkle 2 tablespoons of the ice water over the flour mixture, tossing with a fork; add just enough of the remaining water, by the tablespoon, tossing, so that the dough holds together. Flatten into a disk and wrap in plastic wrap. Refrigerate for 1 hour.

2. Preheat the oven to 425°. On a lightly floured surface, with a lightly floured rolling pin, roll out the dough into an 11-inch circle. Fit into a 9-inch pie plate. Fold the edge under to make a stand-up edge; crimp. Prick the bottom all over with a fork.

3. Bake in the 425° oven until golden brown, 12 to 14 minutes. Remove the pie plate to a wire rack to cool.

4. *Meanwhile, make the filling:* In a heatproof bowl, lightly beat the egg yolks to break up, and then set aside. In a small, heavy saucepan, stir together the sugar, flour, and salt. Gradually stir in

the scalded milk. Cook over medium-low heat, whisking, until thickened and bubbly, 6 to 8 minutes. Stir a little of the hot mixture into the yolks. Stir the yolk mixture back into the saucepan. Heat over very low heat, stirring, for 2 minutes, and do not let boil. Remove the saucepan from the heat. Whisk in the chocolate, butter, and vanilla until melted and smooth. Scrape into a clean bowl. Press a piece of plastic wrap directly on the surface of the filling and let cool for 10 minutes. Remove the plastic wrap and scrape the filling into the pie crust. Cool on a wire rack.

5. Lower the oven to 350°.

6. *Make the meringue:* In a small saucepan, stir together the cornstarch, 2 tablespoons of the sugar, and the water. Cook over medium heat, stirring occasionally, until the mixture comes to a simmer and thickens, 2 to 3 minutes. Remove the saucepan from the heat.

7. In a large bowl, add the salt to the egg whites. With an electric mixer at medium speed, beat just until soft peaks form. Add the cornstarch mixture and beat until creamy. Gradually beat in the remaining sugar and continue to beat until soft peaks form, 6 to 8 minutes.

8. Spread the meringue mixture over the cooled chocolate filling, making sure the meringue touches the pie crust edge all the way around.

9. Bake in the preheated 350° oven until the meringue is golden and its internal temperature registers 150° on an instant-read thermometer, 25 to 30 minutes. Serve soon after. Cover and refrigerate any leftovers.

Sugar Cookies

I was lucky growing up. I never had to buy lunch in the school cafeteria since Mom made me a brown-bag lunch every day. The other kids were always wanting to trade for my homemade cookies. Mom had a whole bunch of cookie cutters for each season and holiday. She would make dough for sugar cookies and let us cut it into bunnies for Easter, hearts for Valentine's Day, and lots of different shapes for Christmas. My brothers and sister and I loved to decorate them with colored icings. Nowadays we sometimes bake sugar cookies to drop off on Christmas Eve at our small-town police and fire departments, and I've already started letting my grandson Elijah help with the decorating.

MAKES 3 TO 3 1/2 DOZEN COOKIES

1 stick or ½ cup butter, at room temperature
⅔ cup sugar
2 large eggs
1 tablespoon vanilla extract
2 cups all-purpose flour
1½ teaspoons baking powder
½ teaspoon salt

1. In a medium bowl with an electric mixer at medium speed, beat the butter until smooth and creamy, about 3 minutes. Gradually beat in the sugar until light and fluffy, 3 to 4 minutes. Beat in the eggs and vanilla.

2. Onto a sheet of waxed paper, sift together the flour, baking powder, and salt. On low speed, beat the flour mixture into the butter mixture until well blended. Flatten the dough into a ½-inch-thick disk. Place on a plate, cover with plastic wrap, and refrigerate until thoroughly chilled, about 3 hours.

3. To bake, preheat the oven to 375°.

4. On a lightly floured work surface, with a lightly floured rolling pin, roll out the dough to ⅛-inch thickness. Using 2½- to 3-inch cookie cutters, cut out cookies into desired shapes. Gather the scraps together, reroll, and cut out more cookies. Place on ungreased baking sheets.

5. Bake in the 375° oven until lightly golden, 8 to 10 minutes. Cool 1 to 2 minutes on the baking sheets on wire racks. Transfer the cookies to the racks to cool. Store in an airtight container.

Lip-Smackin' Snackin'

I made most of my kids' snacks when they were growing up. I could usually coerce them to do their chores if I made this special treat called Chrispy Crusts. I rolled out extra pie crust very thin, cut it into shapes, spread softened butter on the pieces, and then sprinkled them with a little sugar and cinnamon. I'd bake them on a baking sheet, and they'd barely be out of the oven before Wy and Ashley would snatch them up. They thought I had invented these especially for them. But it's an old family "bribe" recipe.

Food fight! Wy didn't duck fast enough.

Back to the Future

Today is June 21, 1997, Grace Pauline Judd Kelley's first birthday. I used to tell Wy that the only way she can fully understand how much I love her is when she has her own. Now, my thirty-three-year-old "little girl," who used to hide her peas in her milk, completely understands.

When someone asked me what's the best part of being a grandparent, I responded, "It's having more time to enjoy the kids than when you were a frantic parent, and having the wisdom to understand just how important and magical a time it is." You and I can't go back and experience the wonders of our childhood or our children's, but we get a third chance to see it again through the eyes of our children's children. Every child born into this world is a new thought of God, an ever-fresh and radiant possibility.

I smile with tears in my eyes as I watch my own happy little Gracie learning to walk. For her birthday party, she's wearing tiny pearl earrings in her pierced ears and clutching a blue patent-leather purse with a heart on it. She takes a couple of steps, then stumbles and falls backward. Sometimes she lands on something hard or bumps her head. She even pulls things down on top of herself. Gracie doesn't mind how awkward she looks or that we were all laughing. She just keeps getting up and trying again. Just like you and me.

Never give up.

These are my reasons to cook:

love,

nutrition,

tradition,

and

Celebration

- **Eat, Relax, and Unite**   • **Thanksgiving**   • **Fourth of July**   • **Halloween**
- **Christmas**   • **Milestones**

EAT, RELAX, AND UNITE

Since food, fun, family, and friends are so important to us Judds, we seize every opportunity to celebrate. We gather to observe all the holidays, to commemorate family events and religious rites, and just for jamborees of noisy merrymaking and uninhibited fun.

Guess what Americans named as their number-one stressor?
The holidays! Get realistic and decide yourself the kind
of holiday you want.

THANKSGIVING

We have a covenant to show up at Mom's for Thanksgiving. One year we even said no to being the Grand Marshals in the Macy's Thanksgiving Day parade in New York City. Another year we turned down an offer to do a big gig at Caesar's Palace in Vegas. We place a high priority on a few days getting away from it all—cooking, eating, and relaxing.

Fans know we're just normal folks and are always accessible to them. Our family has to share us with the whole world year-round, but when so many fans started coming to Mom's kitchen door in droves, my handyman stepdad Wib made a sign for the front yard, saying, "Please Respect Family Time—No Visitors."

The big joke during this holiday is that if we can't find Mom around the house, we always know where she is. Wy telephoned Nana from her bus on her way to Ashland last year, but no one answered at the house. Wy knew she must be at the Kroger store, so she called there and had her paged. Sure enough—she was in aisle thirteen, picking up more groceries and visiting with townspeople.

"I have three chairs in my house—one for solitude, two for company, and three for society."

—HENRY DAVID THOREAU

Never go grocery shopping when you're hungry, 'cause you'll buy too much!

Cornbread Dressing

Say no to surfing the net, TV, deadlines, and controlling people. Say yes to self-reflection, well-loved children, and a strong marriage.

This is a must-have with turkey or chicken. Weeks before Thanksgiving, my Mom makes two 10-inch skillets of cornbread. After they cool, she wraps them well and puts them in the freezer. She also saves stale white bread, biscuits, or rolls, cuts the crusts off and freezes the rest. For her dressing, she uses about one-third as much white bread as cornbread. The average American stuffs him- or herself to the tune of five pounds over the holidays. Guess what the number-one New Year's resolution is?

MAKES 17 CUPS,
ENOUGH TO STUFF A
15- TO 20-POUND BIRD

1 stick or ½ cup butter
2 cups finely chopped celery
2 cups very finely chopped onion
16 cups crumbled cornbread
5 cups crumbled white bread, a day old or lightly toasted
2½ to 3 cups cooled giblet broth or canned chicken broth
1 teaspoon salt
1 teaspoon black pepper
2 tablespoons chopped fresh sage or 4 teaspoons dried leaf sage, crumbled
1 tablespoon dried rosemary, crushed

1. In a large skillet, heat the butter. Add the celery and onion and sauté until softened, about 12 minutes. Transfer to a bowl and let cool.

2. In a large bowl, toss together the cornbread and white bread. Drizzle in the broth, tossing lightly; use just enough broth to make the mixture very moist, but not soggy. (Make sure the liquid is cool, or the stuffing mixture will become glumpy.) Add the salt, pepper, sage, and rosemary. Taste, and adjust the seasonings according to your own taste.

3. Stuff the turkey. Or spoon the stuffing into a buttered 13 × 9 × 3-inch baking dish, drizzle the stuffing with about ½ cup of the broth, and then cover the dish with aluminum foil and bake in a 350° oven for 1 hour. For a crispy top, uncover for the last 15 minutes.

Roast Turkey Tips

These are my Mom's special tips for a flavorful Thanksgiving turkey.

"First, I put the bird on its back. Then I lift the skin at the neck cavity away from the flesh, and with a handful of softened butter or a butter blend, I gently separate the skin from the meat, and put my hand underneath the skin, working it back and forth, spreading butter as I go. I try to cover all the meat on the breast, and then work it over the thighs. Sometimes I'll mix crushed dried rosemary, salt and pepper, and a little lemon juice with the butter. You can use any combination of flavors, making it zesty, smoky, or whatever. As the bird roasts, I continue to baste it on the outside. I cover the bird to keep it moist during the roasting, and then uncover it for the last 15 or 20 minutes so the skin will brown and crisp up."

Potato Pointers

Here's another tip from my Mom: "Some of you may already know this—heating together milk and butter before adding it to the mashed potatoes makes for creamier whipped potatoes, and they stay hot."

Congealed Cranberry Salad with Poppy Seed Dressing

MAKES 10 TO 12 SERVINGS

1 large can (20 ounces) crushed
  pineapple, packed in juice
1 box (6 ounces) strawberry gelatin
1 cup water
1 can (16 ounces) whole-berry
  cranberry sauce
3 tablespoons fresh lemon juice
Poppy Seed Dressing (recipe follows)

1. Drain the pineapple well, reserving all
   the juice and pineapple separately.

2. In a 2-quart saucepan, stir together the
   pineapple juice, gelatin, and water.
   Bring to a boil, stirring to dissolve the
   gelatin. Remove from the heat. Stir in
   the cranberry sauce until well blended.
   Stir in the lemon juice.

3. Transfer the gelatin mixture to a large
   metal bowl. Half-fill a larger bowl with
   ice cubes and cold water. Set the bowl
   with the gelatin in the ice bath. Stir the
   gelatin occasionally with a rubber spatula until the mixture is as thick as
   unbeaten egg whites, about 10 minutes. Remove the bowl of gelatin from
   the ice bath. Fold in the pineapple.

Rinse out a 2-quart decorative mold
with cold water. Pour in the gelatin
mixture. Cover and refrigerate until
firm, about 4 hours.

4. To unmold, dip the mold up to the rim
   in warm (not hot) water for about
   10 seconds. Invert a serving plate over
   the mold, then invert the plate and
   mold together, shaking both gently
   from side to side to relax the gelatin.
   Remove the mold. Serve with the
   Poppy Seed Dressing on the side.

Poppy Seed Dressing

MAKES 1 CUP

1 cup mayonnaise or mayonnaise-style
  creamy salad dressing
1 to 2 tablespoons poppy seeds

In a small bowl, mix together the
mayonnaise and poppy seeds. Cover
and refrigerate until well chilled.

Praise and Gratitude Are Good for Us

This lovely thought for gratitude was sent to me by my personal role model Dr. Rachel Remen, who attends Grace Cathedral in San Francisco:

> *We give thanks for places of simplicity and peace.*
> *May we find such places in ourselves.*
>
> *We give thanks for places of refuge and beauty.*
> *May we find such places in ourselves.*
>
> *We give thanks for places of acceptance and belonging.*
> *May we find such places in ourselves.*
>
> *May we begin to mend the outer world*
> *According to the truth of our inner life.*

One of the reasons we love Thanksgiving is that there's no gift-buying or stress. At Mom's made-from-scratch dinner we enjoy a tradition we started years ago. Each one around the table says what he or she is thankful for.

$E = mc^2$

After a 720-calorie meal, your heart must pump an extra 258 quarts of blood—enough to fill your car's gas tank three times over! This is why the number of heart attacks increases in the twenty-four-hour period after big holiday meals.

After food and family, for the third F (fun) we also pass around David Letterman's "Top 10" books. I'm not just saying this to get one of your free hams, Dave.

Squash Casserole

You can assemble this dish ahead and freeze it. Defrost in your microwave oven following the manufacturer's instructions, and then bake as directed in the recipe below.

MAKES **8** TO **10** SERVINGS

- **3 medium zucchini, trimmed and sliced ¼ inch thick**
- **2 medium onions, thinly sliced and separated into rings**
- **3 medium yellow summer squash, trimmed and sliced ¼ inch thick**
- **½ teaspoon salt**
- **⅛ to ¼ teaspoon black pepper**
- **8-ounce chunk American cheese, shredded (2 cups), or 12 individually wrapped slices American cheese**
- **1 cup soft fresh bread crumbs (about 2 slices bread)**

1. Preheat the oven to 350°.

2. In a 13 × 9 × 2-inch baking dish, arrange a layer of zucchini slices over the bottom, topped with a layer of onions, and then a layer of yellow squash. Sprinkle with a little salt and pepper. Sprinkle with 1 cup of the shredded cheese, or layer on 6 slices of cheese. Repeat the layers, ending with the cheese. Sprinkle the top with the bread crumbs.

3. Bake, uncovered, in the 350° oven until the casserole is bubbly, the bread crumbs are browned, and a wooden pick inserted into the squash pieces meets no resistance, about 1 hour. Let stand for 10 minutes before serving.

Sweet Potato Casserole

Or as Popeye says, "I am what I yam!"

MAKES 6 TO 8 SERVINGS

3 cups mashed sweet potatoes
  (about 2 pounds sweet potatoes)
½ cup granulated sugar
2 large eggs, lightly beaten
½ cup milk
½ stick or ¼ cup butter, melted
½ teaspoon salt
½ teaspoon vanilla extract

TOPPING
½ cup packed light brown sugar
½ cup chopped walnuts, pecans,
  or other nuts
⅓ cup all-purpose flour
⅓ cup butter

1. Preheat the oven to 350°. Grease a
   shallow 2-quart casserole.

2. In a medium bowl, stir together the
   potatoes, granulated sugar, eggs, milk,
   butter, salt, and vanilla and scrape the
   mixture into the prepared casserole.

3. *Make the topping:* In a small bowl, stir
   together the brown sugar, nuts, and
   flour. Sprinkle over the top of the
   casserole. Dot with the butter. Place
   the casserole on a baking sheet.

4. Bake, uncovered, in the 350° oven
   until heated through and lightly
   browned, 30 to 35 minutes. Let stand
   10 minutes before serving.

Tricks Are for Kids

At holidays, Uncle Norman used to remove his false teeth to gross out me and my young cousins. Today, Larry is the man with the plan. It began when my sister's son Josh was eight. Larry bent his thumb into the palm of his hand, then held the end of a carrot about the same size as his thumb, in the same spot, and covered it with his napkin. He asked Josh to pull his thumb, then Larry let out a scream just as the carrot under the napkin came off in Josh's hand. Larry did the bent-over-double belly laugh as Joshua shrieked in horror. Next Thanksgiving, Larry put a plastic cup up under his armpit beneath his shirt. Holding his arm close to his chest like it was bothering him, he asked Josh to pull his arm. Josh obliged and Larry squeezed his arm into his chest, causing the cup to crunch. Josh, who believed he had dislocated Uncle Larry's shoulder, ran out of the house screaming, "Gross!"

What's a Chortle?

Can you name the different types of humor? This answer is from a helpful book you'll enjoy, *Managing Stress* by my buddy Brian Luke Seward, Ph.D.: parody, satire, slapstick, absurd/nonsense, black humor, irony, dry humor and puns, and sarcasm. The four categories that describe most folks' sense of humor are: conventional, life of the party, creative, and good sport. Which are you?

Momily: Remember, you're just as good as anybody else. And not a bit better.

Yeast Rolls

All rise. Friends are like elevator buttons—they can take you up or down. Oh yes, the company you keep will determine the trouble you meet.

MAKES 24 ROLLS

½ **cup sugar**
½ **cup warm water (105° to 115°)**
2 **packages active dry yeast**
2 **teaspoons salt**
⅓ **cup solid vegetable shortening**
1 **cup cold water**
1 **egg, well beaten**
4½ **cups all-purpose flour**
2 **tablespoons butter, melted**

1. In a large bowl, add a pinch of sugar to the warm water. Sprinkle the yeast over the top and let stand until foamy, about 5 minutes. Stir to dissolve the yeast.

2. Beat in the remaining sugar, the salt, shortening, cold water, and egg until well blended. On low speed, beat in 2 cups of the flour and beat for 2 minutes. Beat in enough of the remaining flour, ½ cup at a time, to make a soft dough.

3. Place the dough in a well greased bowl and turn to coat the dough. Cover with a towel and let rise in a warm place away from drafts until doubled in bulk, about 1½ hours.

4. Punch the dough down and refrigerate for 2 hours. The dough will almost double in bulk.

5. Grease two 9-inch round cake pans. Turn the dough out onto a floured surface. Pull off pieces of the dough, about a scant ¼ cup each, and shape into 24 rolls. Place 12 rolls, sides touching, in each of the 2 prepared pans. Brush with butter. Let rise in a warm place for 1 hour or until almost doubled.

6. Preheat the oven to 425°.

7. Bake the rolls in the 425° oven until well browned on top, about 15 minutes. Transfer the pans to wire racks to cool for 5 minutes. Transfer the rolls to the racks to cool.

Count your blessings every day.

Wy, Ashley, and I supported each other through struggle, tragedy, and triumph.

Coconut Cake

A cakewalk is actually a promenade in which the couple performing the most intricate steps wins a cake for their prize. I would even do the Big Butt dance in public to win this cake. Well . . . maybe just an interpretive dance to a Judd song?

Mom says: "Be sure to make the frosting ahead to give it time to reach the proper consistency."

MAKES 16 SERVINGS

COCONUT FROSTING

2 cups sour cream
1 bag (7 ounces) flaked sweetened coconut
1¼ cups sugar

CAKES

Nonstick vegetable cooking spray
2¾ cups cake flour
1 tablespoon baking powder
½ teaspoon salt
1½ sticks or ¾ cup unsalted butter, at room temperature
1½ cups sugar
4 large eggs
2 teaspoons vanilla extract
1 cup milk

1. *Make the frosting:* In a large bowl, combine the sour cream, coconut, and sugar and stir just until blended. Cover the bowl and refrigerate the frosting overnight.

2. *On the second day, make the cakes:* Preheat the oven to 350°. Coat two 9-inch round cake pans with cooking spray. Line bottoms of the pans with circles of waxed paper. Coat paper with spray and dust the pans with flour, tapping out excess flour.

3. Into a medium bowl, sift together the cake flour, baking powder, and salt. In a large bowl, with an electric mixer on medium speed, beat the butter until smooth and creamy, about 2 minutes. Gradually beat in the sugar and beat for 2 minutes until light and fluffy. Beat in the eggs, one at a time, until well blended. Beat in the vanilla. On low speed, beat in the flour mixture in thirds, alternately with the milk, beginning and ending with the flour, until blended. Divide the batter between the pans and spread evenly.

4. Bake in the 350° oven until a wooden pick inserted in the centers comes out clean, 30 to 35 minutes. Let the cakes cool in the pans on wire racks for 10 minutes. Turn the cakes out onto the racks. Turn right side up, remove the waxed paper, and cool completely. Split the cakes in half horizontally with a serrated knife.

5. Place one bottom cake layer, cut-side up, on a serving plate. Spread with ¾ cup frosting. Cover with a top cake layer, cut-side down. Spread with another ¾ cup frosting. Top with remaining bottom layer, another ¾ cup frosting, and remaining top cake layer. Spread the remaining frosting over the top and sides of the cake. The frosting will be thin. Serve the cake right away or refrigerate until serving time.

Smart cookies don't crumble.

Mom says, "When things
are bad and getting worse,
keep a cookie in your purse."

Apricot Cookie Rolls

MAKES 64 COOKIES

2 sticks or 1 cup unsalted butter,
at room temperature

1 container (8 ounces) sour cream

½ teaspoon salt

2 cups all-purpose flour

¾ cup flaked sweetened coconut

¾ cup chopped pecans

¾ cup apricot preserves

Confectioners' sugar, for dusting
(optional)

1. In a medium bowl with an electric mixer on medium speed, beat the butter until fluffy, about 2 minutes. Beat in the sour cream and salt. On low speed, beat in the flour to make a soft dough. Divide the dough into fourths. Wrap each in plastic wrap and refrigerate until firm and well chilled, at least 4 hours.

2. In a small bowl, stir together the coconut, pecans, and preserves.

3. Place an oven rack in the upper third of the oven. Preheat the oven to 350°. Grease several baking sheets.

4. Place one-quarter of the dough on a well-floured surface, keeping the remainder chilled. With a lightly floured rolling pin, roll the dough out to a 9½ × 9½-inch square, about ⅛ inch thick. Trim the edges even. Cut into sixteen 2-inch squares. Shape the scraps into little cookies for nibbling. Spread 1 teaspoon of the apricot mixture in the center of each square. Moisten two opposite corners with water. Starting at one moistened corner, roll up the square diagonally to the opposite corner. Moisten the seam with water and press to seal. Place, seam side up, on the prepared baking sheets, along with the "scrap" cookies.

5. Repeat with the remaining dough and filling.

6. Bake, one sheet at a time, in upper third of the 350° oven until lightly browned, 18 to 20 minutes. Transfer the cookies to wire racks to cool.

7. To serve, sprinkle with confectioners' sugar, if desired. Store in tightly covered containers.

The mother-daughter relationship is the most complicated. Mom and I once went years without speaking.

Freedom also means you can wear
goofy hats in public.

FOURTH OF JULY

Our Fourth of July picnic is no place for folks who are not proud of their country. Our godson Casey holds up a big flag as about forty of our family and friends recite the Pledge of Allegiance and read the Declaration of Independence, which I have printed for all. We even sing "The Star-Spangled Banner" and "God Bless America" while watching the sunset by the lake. After it gets dark, we ooh! and ahh! at fireworks through 3-D glasses.

Happy Birthday, America!

There's much carrying on and joke-telling at our Fourth of July picnics. This is one of my favorites: A campaigning politician seeking votes visits a senior-citizen home and walks over to a little old lady sitting in a wheelchair and asks, "Hello, do you know who I am?" "No," she replies. "But maybe if you go down to the office, somebody there can tell you."

Larry has the most realistic-looking life-size snake on our driveway waiting to scare the daylights out of visitors. He calls it his guard snake. No, it doesn't bark a warning like a dog. Instead, approaching visitors scream as soon as they spot the snake, and thereby announce themselves.

Larry has a fake arm and leg he lets stick out of the blades of the mower on our tractor in our pasture. He likes to take new visitors on walks and watch them as they approach the tractor, squint their eyes, and mutter, "Oh, my God!"

Parades

I love a parade because it brings out the community spirit. When I was little, my brothers, sister, and I would watch our hometown parade, sitting on the curb in front of Daddy's station on our main street. We'd sip Nehi grape sodas from Dad's big blue pop cooler and crane our necks watching for the Shriners in their teeny cars.

Now that we have grandchildren, it is even more fun to take them to the parades on Main Street in our small friendly town of Franklin. My husband, who's six feet tall and very much a man's man, becomes another person at parades. He's been known to walk up to total strangers and ask them if he might sit on their shoulders so he can see better. Sometimes when the big float comes by, he cups his hands and yells at the top of his lungs, "Hit the sidewalk, she's gonna blow!" My friend Jay Leno told me that he once went out on a Sunday afternoon to drive one of his gazillion old cars down Santa Monica Boulevard and unknowingly made a turn into the Gay Pride Parade! That really started tongues wagging.

I think life can be compared to a parade: There has to be a Grand Marshal, somebody who's in charge. Then there are always baton-twirling majorettes who enjoy being out front; marchers who obey commands and stay within the lines; and those who are content to sit on the curb and watch it all as it passes them by.

A shut mouth gathers no foot: Language is the expression of your thoughts. Every time you open your mouth, your mind is on parade.

Colors, sounds, movement—Grace and Elijah want to be in a parade!

The rising tide lifts all

boats equally.

Southern Sausage-Ball Appetizers

My Mom has used this recipe for parties at home as well as parties she's catered since Lincoln was President. These can be made ahead, frozen unbaked, and then baked in a 400° oven for 15 minutes.

Do you know what Abraham Lincoln, Martin Luther King, and George Washington all had in common? They were all born on holidays. Wy was born on Memorial Day and was seven years old when a classmate finally burst her bubble and explained it wasn't a national holiday just because it was her birthday.

**MAKES ABOUT
40 SAUSAGE BALLS**

1 pound hot bulk sausage
**2 cups (8 ounces) shredded sharp
  Cheddar cheese**
2 cups all-purpose flour
3 tablespoons finely chopped onion
2 tablespoons chopped fresh parsley
2 teaspoons dried poultry seasoning
1½ teaspoons baking powder

1. Preheat the oven to 400°.

2. In a medium bowl, combine all the ingredients with your hands and mix thoroughly but lightly, avoiding mashing the meat together too much. Pick off pieces of meat mixture the size of a walnut, about 1 level tablespoon, and shape into balls. Place on an ungreased baking sheet, preferably with sides to catch any fat that may drizzle off the sheet.

3. Bake in the 400° oven until the balls are cooked through, about 12 minutes. Serve hot.

Whatever Pimiento Cheese Spread

Serve this as a spread for crackers, or in a little crock as a dip for a platter of cut-up fresh vegetables.

MAKES ABOUT 3 CUPS

**8 ounces sharp Cheddar cheese,
  preshredded or cut into chunks**
**4 ounces Colby or similar mild cheese,
  cut into chunks**
**¼ teaspoon ground hot-red pepper
  (cayenne)**
**¼ cup mayonnaise-style creamy salad
  dressing**
**1 jar (4 ounces) diced pimientos, well
  drained**
½ cup sweet pickle relish
1 tablespoon finely chopped onion
Few drops hot sauce (optional)
**Chopped green olives, stuffed or
  unstuffed, to taste (optional)**

1. In a food processor, combine the Cheddar cheese, Colby, and red pepper. Pulse to chop and combine.

2. With the motor running, add a small amount of the salad dressing to make the mixture smooth. Add the pimientos and process until smooth.

3. Add more of the remaining salad dressing until the mixture is spreadable. Add the relish and onion. Pulse to combine. Add a drop or two of the hot sauce and/or chopped green olives, if you'd like. Pulse to combine.

Lost-and-Found Department

Lookin' for some plain ol' common sense? I always do. I have an intense attraction to basic values. A recent poll in *USA Today Weekend* shows an overwhelming majority of Americans believe in the importance of personal responsibility, family ties, a spiritual life, a strong work ethic, and the need for charity. But the poll also found seventy-nine percent of Americans agree there's still racial discrimination. Fight prejudice and discrimination wherever you find it. Don't be afraid to let what you stand for be known as well as what you won't stand for. Information is our most valuable tool in dealing with any reality. Find out about the issues, then vote!

Generally Speaking

General Norman Schwarzkopf and I were speaking at the same event when I heard him say, "The truth of the matter is you always know what to do. The hard part is doing it."

I recently enjoyed chatting with Alma and Colin Powell. Colin believes our gift of freedom must be tempered with personal responsibility, so he's involved in promoting volunteerism. It's obvious he and Alma believe in the power of love instead of the love of power. I've always thought the reason to gain power is so you can give it away. Its only purpose should be to help others.

Instead of asking someone what they do for a living, ask, "What have you done that you believe in and are proud of?"

Lime Jell-O Salad

Another "congealed' salad. These salads have a long tradition in the South. Since the weather is warm more often than not, these kinds of cooling foods are refreshing.

MAKES **8** SERVINGS

3 cups water

1 box (6 ounces) lime Jell-O

1 package (8 ounces) cream cheese, at room temperature

1 can (8 ounces) crushed pineapple packed in juice, drained

½ cup chopped walnuts

Green leafy lettuce, for serving

1. In a medium saucepan, bring the 3 cups of water to a boil. Stir in the Jell-O until dissolved. Remove from the heat. Whisk in the cream cheese until well blended. Stir in the pineapple and nuts.

2. Pour into a 6-cup mold or bowl, or eight ½-cup individual molds. Refrigerate until firm, about 4 hours. Unmold. Serve on a bed of lettuce with Dr. Seuss's favorite meal, *Green Eggs and Ham.*

Cucumber and Onion Salad

After Wilbert Rideout and my Mom were married, Mom retired from cooking on Wilbert's towboat and cooked just for the family. This is one of Wilbert's favorites, except he picks out the cucumber slices since they don't agree with him. Try spooning this over sliced tomatoes. My Mom talks about food as passionately as Wy talks about music, Ashley movies, and me everything. I recently heard Mom and my Aunt Roberta, sitting at our kitchen table, discussing the different varieties of cucumbers for forty-five minutes. Whatever floats your boat!

MAKES 6 SERVINGS

3 large cucumbers, peeled

**3 medium Vidalia or other sweet
   onions**

DRESSING

1 cup water

¾ cup vegetable oil

⅓ cup sugar

¼ cup cider vinegar

1 teaspoon dried tarragon

¾ teaspoon salt

**½ teaspoon white pepper or black
   pepper**

1. Slice the cucumbers and onions ¼ inch thick. Combine in a large bowl with a tight-fitting lid.

2. *Make the dressing:* In a medium enameled (not metal) pot, combine all the dressing ingredients. Bring to a boil, stirring, over medium heat. Boil for 3 minutes. Immediately pour over the cucumbers and onions. Cover and refrigerate. Serve well chilled. This will keep, refrigerated, for up to 2 weeks.

Cucumbers for Breakfast

Having to look good on a movie set early in the A.M., Ashley has had to find a fix-it for puffy, tired eyes. Through trial and error, she's discovered that cold cucumber slices placed directly over the eyes work as an astringent, and feel great. Ashley says that 1 teaspoon of freshly grated horseradish, eaten directly, helps to relieve her sinus stuffiness. It also makes her gag!

Time Savors—Relieve Holiday or Everyday Stress

Hey you—stop right there! Put your hands in the air and no one will get hurt. Now, clasp them together over your head and slowly stretch upward. Then clasp your hands together behind your back and do the same. During my day, I'll stop whatever I'm doing for five to ten minutes of stretches. Feels so-o-o good.

Take tennis shoes to work and take a walk on your break. Take deep cleansing breaths—in through the nose and out through the mouth. We don't realize how shallow we're breathing until we focus our attention on it. The quickest way to center ourselves in the moment is to concentrate on our breathing.

Step away from your work and look at a magazine, chat with a co-worker, or call a friend. The minute you come home from work, change into something casual. Leave thoughts of work outside when you close your door.

Marriage is based on three things— trust, respect, commitment.

Behind every successful

woman . . .

is herself!

If you're at home during the day, take time out to play with your pet. Doing laundry is my favorite housework. When I'm taking warm towels out of the dryer, I bury my face in them and wrap them around my neck. Step outside and walk around in your yard. Really feel the warmth of the sun on your face. I lie on a quilt on the ground in my backyard to feel the earth supporting me. Go out at night and look at your home with the lights on.

When I'm traveling, I carry two aromatherapy oils and dot them on my wrist. Eucalyptus clears your nasal passages and lavender promotes relaxation. I did this in a big meeting and wound up passing them around for everyone to try!

I highly recommend you try massage. If you can't afford it, do like I used to do—barter. Find out what personal service you can do for the massage therapist: baby-sit his or her kids, run errands, cook a meal, whatever. Yoga is wonderful for breaks and for doing something good for yourself. Yoga, which means unity (spirit, mind, body), not only helps to make you more flexible and stronger, but calms and centers you. It is *not* a religion, it's a science. Treat yourself to a retreat or workshop on wellness. Everybody in your family will reap the rewards along with you.

Celebrate yourself by taking a pause for the cause. No matter what you're doing—working or playing—stop to enjoy yourself.

Take Time to Meet Your Neighbors

When I was growing up, every July the old folks' home on the corner of our block held an ice cream social. It was always in July, so the weather was warm and balmy. They had Chinese lanterns and long tables set out on their front lawn. This was one of my favorite parts of childhood. All the neighbors came out of their houses to socialize for that evening. Homemade ice cream was my favorite food, so I blew a month's allowance. Being nourished by the friendly company of our neighborhood was as satisfying as the delicious ice cream in my mouth.

Life is like tennis—to win you need to learn to serve.

The food drive in my hometown Ashland, Kentucky, is about neighbor helping neighbor and community spirit.

Rice-a-Roni Salad

This recipe comes from Holly and Helen who cooked for us when Wynonna and I were appearing at Lake Tahoe.

MAKES 8 SERVINGS

1 box (6.9 ounces) chicken-flavored Rice-a-Roni, cooked according to package directions and refrigerated until cold

2 jars (6 ounces each) marinated artichoke hearts, drained, marinade reserved, and artichokes cut into small pieces

2 green onions, chopped

1 can (8 ounces) sliced water chestnuts, drained

12 to 16 stuffed green olives, sliced (about ¼ cup)

⅓ cup mayonnaise

¼ teaspoon curry powder

1. In a large bowl, combine the cooked rice, cut-up artichoke hearts, green onions, water chestnuts, and olives.

2. In a small bowl, whisk together the reserved artichoke marinade, the mayonnaise, and curry powder. With a rubber spatula, fold the mayonnaise mixture into the rice mixture until thoroughly blended. Cover and refrigerate until well chilled.

Kraut Salad

Red head, red head, five cents a cabbage head. Cabbage contains glutamine, an amino acid shown to heal ulcers. If you have a flare-up, try at least one healthy serving every day for two weeks. Kids get ulcers, too, from stress, disease, allergic reactions to drugs, and bacterial infections.

MAKES 4 TO 6 SERVINGS

- **1 refrigerated bag (32 ounces) sauerkraut, rinsed and drained**
- **1 large onion, minced**
- **1 green bell pepper, minced**
- **3 stalks celery, minced**
- **2 cups sugar**
- **1 jar (2 ounces) minced pimiento, drained**

In a medium bowl, mix all the ingredients together. Refrigerate, well covered, in a glass container for up to 2 weeks.

The Best Lemon Pie

This is another one of my Mom's best.
To top it off—pun intended—just add
Mama's foolproof meringue from the
Chocolate Meringue Pie (page 152).

MAKES **8** SERVINGS

LEMON FILLING

3 large egg yolks

1½ cups sugar

7 tablespoons cornstarch

¼ teaspoon salt

1½ cups hot water

½ cup fresh lemon juice

2 tablespoons butter or margarine

One 9-inch baked pie shell

1. *Make the filling:* In a heatproof bowl,
   lightly beat the egg yolks to break them
   up, and then set aside.

2. In a medium, heavy saucepan, stir
   together the sugar, cornstarch, and salt.
   Stir in the hot water until smooth.
   Bring to a boil over high heat, stirring.
   When the mixture begins to thicken,
   reduce the heat to medium-low and
   cook, stirring, at a very gentle boil for
   5 minutes. Remove the saucepan from
   the heat. Stir several spoonfuls into the
   yolks. Stir this yolk mixture into the

sugar mixture in the saucepan. Cook
over low heat, stirring until thickened
and bubbly, 3 to 5 minutes.

3. Remove the saucepan from the heat.
   Stir in the lemon juice and butter.
   Place a piece of waxed paper directly

on the surface of the filling and let the
saucepan cool on a wire rack.

4. Remove the waxed paper and spoon
   the cooled filling into the baked pie
   shell. Serve, or cover and refrigerate for
   up to a day.

HALLOWEEN

Autumn is my favorite time of year, so we love to have fall festivals at Wy's lake. Since we consider those who work at our office, The Judd House, our friends, we try to have get-togethers when we don't talk business. This year we had somebody dressed like a scarecrow slump in a chair with a basket of candy in his lap. When arrivees leaned down to take a treat, scarecrow would grab them and let out a whoop! Those who'd already "been had" particularly enjoyed watching new initiates.

Have you ever sat around a bonfire on a fall night? It's one of my favorite nature experiences. I do an intro to a scary story, then we go around the circle, having each person string on a line to further the plot of the ghost story while holding a flashlight under their chin to create an eerie effect. The highlight of the night, second only to the great food, is the Haunted Path. We position men dressed as ghouls along a path in our woods. The climax is the last man disguised in a camouflage suit with pantyhose over his head. Oh yeah, I almost forgot—he holds a smoking chain saw!

A fall tradition is taking Elijah to pick out his pumpkin at Earl's Fruit Stand.

For our parties, you don't dress up or stand around with a drink in your hand, asking somebody what sign they are.

Favorite Easy Chili

Delicious with Fried Corncakes (recipe follows) or Mexican Cornbread (page 132).

MAKES 6 SERVINGS (12 CUPS)

1 tablespoon vegetable oil
1 large onion, diced
1 green bell pepper, cored, seeded, and diced (optional)
1 pound lean ground beef round
2 tablespoons chili powder
2 teaspoons salt
1 teaspoon black pepper
5 teaspoons flour
Hot water
3 cans (10¼ ounces each) condensed tomato soup
3 cans (15½ ounces each) kidney beans, undrained
1 can (16 ounces) stewed tomatoes
Garnishes (optional): Grated Monterey Jack cheese or other cheese, chopped onion or green onion, snipped fresh chives, and sour cream

1. In a 4-quart saucepan or Dutch oven over medium-high heat, heat the oil. Add the onion and the green pepper, if using; cook, stirring, until softened, about 10 minutes.

2. Add the beef, breaking up clumps with a wooden spoon, and cook until browned, about 15 minutes.

3. Meanwhile, in a small bowl, stir together the chili powder, salt, pepper, and flour. Stir in just enough hot water to make a smooth paste.

4. Into the meat mixture, stir in the soup, beans, and tomatoes. Bring to a boil. Lower the heat. Stir in the chili powder mixture. Cover and let simmer for 30 minutes, stirring frequently to prevent scorching on the bottom.

5. Pass the bowls of garnishes at the table, if using.

Fried Corncakes

Serve hot with big steaming bowls of soup or chili.

MAKES ABOUT 36 CORNCAKES

2 cups self-rising yellow cornmeal*
¾ cup self-rising flour*
¼ cup sugar
1 large egg
1¾ cups water
Melted butter or nonstick cooking spray, for the skillet

1. In a large mixing bowl, ideally with a pouring spout, stir together the cornmeal, flour, and sugar until well blended. Make a well in the center and add the egg and water, and then stir it all together to make a pancake-like batter.

2. Heat a medium, heavy skillet over medium-high heat. Brush with butter or lightly coat with nonstick cooking spray.

3. Into the skillet, pour about 1 tablespoon batter for each 3-inch corncake, 3 or 4 at a time, taking care that they don't touch. Cook until lightly browned, about 1 minute. Flip over and cook the second sides until golden, about 1 minute. Serve immediately while still steaming hot.

★ TIP
Instead of the self-rising cornmeal and self-rising flour, you can use the same amount of regular yellow cornmeal and the same amount of regular all-purpose flour. Just add 4 teaspoons of baking powder and 1¼ teaspoons of salt with the dry ingredients.

CHRISTMAS

This is a copy of a letter to the editor that was printed in December 1996 in our newspaper *The Tennessean*.

Dear Fellow Nashvillians,

Our family wants to wish all of you a Merry Christmas.

About six years ago, I became so fed up with the commercialization of Christmas, I called a family powwow. Christmas has become the most stressful time of the year. We stew in traffic, grumble in long lines at the mall to buy gifts for people who don't need anything and enslave ourselves to tasks for which we don't have time. Some folks even go into debt. I have become increasingly concerned about the unrealistic expectations of Christmas the media projects. These preposterous images of the perfect family sitting around the perfect tree in the perfect house. No such things exist.

We decided to take Christmas back. We now spend our time doing for others, relaxing at home with our family and visiting with friends. Christmas is once again what it was meant to be.

You've heard it said before, "Jesus is the reason for the Season." Join us in celebrating the birth of our savior, the Prince of Peace. Our wish for you is that you might fully understand the gift that you've already been given.

—Naomi Judd

Don't fall into holiday traps. Christmas should be an enjoyable time of spiritual renewal. Ashley, me, Grace, Wy, and Elijah are talking with a special friend.

Hot Fruit Punch

MAKES **1** QUART

3 cinnamon sticks
1 tablespoon whole cloves
1½ teaspoons whole allspice
2¼ cups pineapple juice
2 cups cranberry juice
1¾ cups water
½ cup packed brown sugar
⅛ teaspoon salt

1. In the coffee basket of a glass percolator, place the cinnamon sticks, cloves, and allspice.

2. In the percolator, stir together the pineapple juice, cranberry juice, water, brown sugar, and salt to dissolve the sugar.

3. Place the percolator, covered, over medium-high heat and bring to a boil. Perk for 5 minutes. Serve hot.

Cheese Wafers

This recipe comes through Mom, who got it from Vivian Bradley, who catered many parties over the years in Ashland, Kentucky.

When I was a kid, Mom would make these wafers for very special occasions—definitely at Christmastime. We didn't have many special events, so when these appeared, we knew to relish the moment. Such fancy touches were limited then. But these wafers were certainly one of them. Later as an adult, I remember being in a gourmet food store and seeing these for sale at some exorbitant price.

MAKES ABOUT 6 DOZEN WAFERS IF SLICED, OR ABOUT 8 DOZEN IF USING A COOKIE PRESS

1 pound New York State sharp Cheddar cheese

2 sticks or 1 cup butter, at room temperature

2 cups all-purpose flour

1 teaspoon salt

½ teaspoon ground hot-red pepper (cayenne), or less if you like your food a little less spicy

Pecan halves, one for each wafer

1. Into a medium bowl, grate the cheese. Mash in the butter until well combined. Mix in the flour, salt, and pepper until a smooth dough is formed.

2. Shape the mixture into 2 logs, 9½ × 1½ inches.★ Place in the refrigerator until well chilled, about 2 hours.

3. To bake, preheat the oven to 350°.

4. Cut the log into ¼-inch-thick slices and place the slices on ungreased baking sheets. Place a pecan half on top of each.

5. Bake in the 350° oven until lightly colored, about 12 minutes. Watch very carefully, since these can scorch very quickly. Transfer the baking sheets to wire racks to cool slightly. Transfer the wafers to the racks to cool.

★ NOTE

You can also put the wafer dough in a cookie press fitted with a spritz cookie plate. In this case, do not refrigerate the dough. Press out onto ungreased baking sheets. Place a pecan half on each.

Granny's Chicken Spaghetti Casserole

If you're looking for an easy entree to fix during the busy holiday time, this is it. Everybody likes it—it's hot and hearty. We have a large extended family. Larry and I fell in love eight years ago with Casey Robertson from our church, who was then seven, and we've enjoyed having him spend weekends and summers with us ever since. And then there's Ashley's best friend Mary Tripp Reid, who's so at home at Peaceful Valley, she's even been in some of our powwows. This yummy casserole comes from Mary's Granny Reid over in Arkansas.

MAKES 8 SERVINGS, OR FEEDS 1 SUMO WRESTLER

1 can (10¼ ounces) condensed tomato soup, undiluted

1 can (10¼ ounces) condensed mushroom soup, undiluted

1 can (13¾ ounces) chicken broth

1 tablespoon Worcestershire sauce

1 small onion, diced

1 clove garlic, chopped

Nonstick cooking spray, for the baking dish

1 pound vermicelli, cooked

3 or 4 medium whole chicken breasts, cooked, bone and skin removed and chicken shredded

¾ cup chopped canned black olives

¾ pound shredded sharp cheese

1. Preheat the oven to 350°.

2. In medium bowl, stir together the tomato soup, mushroom soup, chicken broth, Worcestershire, onion, and garlic.

3. In a 13 × 9 × 2-inch baking dish, coated with nonstick cooking spray, layer the vermicelli, chicken, and soup mixture. Scatter the olives over the top. Cover with aluminum foil.

4. Bake in the 350° oven for 40 minutes. Sprinkle with the shredded cheese. Bake, uncovered, another 5 minutes or until cheese is melted.

Create Your Own Traditions and Ceremonies

The year we took back Christmas, we got a group of friends together and went to an inner-city church in Nashville, where we helped prepare a hearty holiday dinner for twenty-four homeless people. We gave them warm clothes, sang carols, and visited. The next day we went to a center for terminally ill children, giving them presents and refreshments and singing their favorite Christmas songs. When we returned home, we looked like anything but the "perfect designer family." The two days made us reflect on our own blessings, and we felt like we acknowledged the reason for the season.

We've been conditioned to feel we have to give gifts for special occasions. This winds up being more for ourselves to avoid guilt than for the recipient of the gift. If you find a special gift and have a creative urge, go ahead. Otherwise, make it honest. If you can, give a present of words—talk to someone about how much they mean to you, give them thanks, share memories, offer them affirmations—or make handmade items, go to an event with this person and share the experience together, give blood, offer to baby-sit for an overworked mother, give new books to the library, help a neighbor in need, take some groceries to a food shelter, do work on a volunteer level at a local soup kitchen or women's shelter. Christmas and other holidays can be either a chore or a treasure. As usual, you get to choose.

Texas Lizzies

These are delicious festive cookies, almost like tiny, tiny fruitcakes. Baking cookies together is one of our oldest family traditions. Wy, Ashley, and I bake batches on Christmas Eve and deliver them to our local sheriff's department. I urge you to teach your kids to respect our law-enforcement officials as well as our teachers, clergy, and the elderly.

MAKES ABOUT 9 DOZEN

- 1 stick or ½ cup butter, at room temperature
- 1 box (16 ounces) light brown sugar
- 4 large eggs
- 3½ cups all-purpose flour
- 3 teaspoons baking soda
- 1 teaspoon ground nutmeg
- 1 teaspoon ground cinnamon
- ½ to ¾ cup whiskey
- ¾ pound walnuts, chopped
- ¾ pound pecans, chopped
- 1 box (15 ounces) golden raisins
- 1¼ cups dark raisins
- 8 ounces red candied cherries, chopped
- 8 ounces green candied cherries, chopped

1. Preheat the oven to 350°. Grease several baking sheets.

2. In a large bowl, with an electric mixer at medium speed, beat the butter until smooth and creamy, about 2 minutes. Beat in the sugar until light and fluffy. Beat in the eggs, one at a time, beating well after each addition.

3. Into another large bowl, sift together the flour, baking soda, nutmeg, and cinnamon.

4. On low speed, beat the flour mixture into the butter mixture alternately with the whiskey, beginning and ending with the flour mixture. Stir in the nuts, raisins, and red and green candied cherries.

5. Onto the prepared baking sheets, drop dough by rounded tablespoons, placing them 2 inches apart.

6. Bake in the 350° oven until set in the center, 10 to 12 minutes. Transfer the lizzies to wire racks to cool. Store in tightly covered containers.

Snickerdoodles

Truth in advertising: These yummy cookies do not contain Snickers, but then Rocky Mountain oysters do not come from the sea. My brothers, sister, and I could always count on these being in the cookie jar at special times of the year.

MAKES ABOUT 6 DOZEN 2-INCH COOKIES

2¾ **cups all-purpose flour**

2 **teaspoons cream of tartar**

1 **teaspoon baking soda**

½ **teaspoon salt**

2 **sticks or 1 cup butter, at room temperature**

1½ **cups sugar**

2 **eggs**

CINNAMON-SUGAR

3 **tablespoons sugar + 1 tablespoon ground cinnamon**

1. Onto a sheet of waxed paper, sift together the flour, cream of tartar, baking soda, and salt.

2. In a medium bowl, beat the butter with an electric mixer at medium speed until smooth and creamy, about 3 minutes. Gradually beat in the sugar until light and fluffy, about 3 minutes. Beat in the eggs until well blended. On low speed, beat in the flour mixture

until well blended. Press the dough into a 1-inch-thick disk. Wrap in waxed paper and refrigerate until thoroughly chilled, about 3 hours.

3. To bake, preheat the oven to 375°.

4. Pick off pieces of the dough the size of a walnut and with your palms roll into balls 1 inch in diameter. Roll in the Cinnamon-Sugar to coat. Place 2 inches apart on an ungreased baking sheet.

5. Bake in the 375° degree oven until light brown but still soft to the touch, 8 to 10 minutes. Transfer the snickerdoodles to wire racks to cool.

MILESTONES

"Cake Is Fire Hazard"

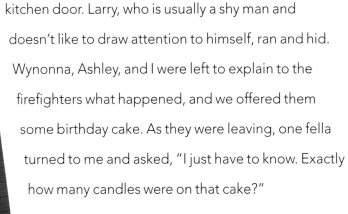

A couple of months ago, the Powwow gathered at Wynonna's house to celebrate Larry's birthday. We were having a wonderful evening of lively family banter. When the cake was brought out, Larry enthusiastically blew out all of his many candles. We were creating such noisy merriment we didn't hear the smoke-detector alarm. But we couldn't miss the sirens from the fire trucks that screamed up to the kitchen door. Larry, who is usually a shy man and doesn't like to draw attention to himself, ran and hid. Wynonna, Ashley, and I were left to explain to the firefighters what happened, and we offered them some birthday cake. As they were leaving, one fella turned to me and asked, "I just have to know. Exactly how many candles were on that cake?"

Franklin's Finest Firemen/Firewoman

We're not getting older . . .

we're just having an

out-of-youth experience.

Children keep us young. My grandchildren are the jewels in my crown.

Birthdays Are a Laughing Matter

Presents are unimportant on my birthday 'cause I feel I've been given the greatest gift already—life.

For my birthday parties, I usually invite family and close friends, and tell them to bring jokes or Gary Larsen cartoons, quotes, and topics for discussion such as "Is there life on other planets?" One of my favorite quotes is from Helen Keller: "The best and most beautiful things in the world cannot be seen or even touched. They must be felt in the heart." Laughter is so important in my life that I even have a special joke club. Here's a joke that's typical of the ones at my party: An old man gets pulled over by the police for speeding. As the cop leans in the window and says, "Sir, you were going over the speed limit," the old man's wife interrupts. "I keep telling him he drives way too fast. I knew this would happen." The old man loudly tells her, "Shut up!" When the officer asks to see his license and registration, she hollers, "He doesn't have a registration and his license is expired." Again, the old man orders her to shut up. Finally the officer turns to the wife and asks, "Ma'am, does he always talk to you like this?" "No," she answers, "only when he's been drinkin'."

Fudge Frosting

Use this frosting for your favorite white or yellow cake recipe.

MAKES 2¼ CUPS, ENOUGH FOR TWO 8- OR 9-INCH LAYERS, OR ONE 13 × 9 × 2-INCH CAKE

- 2 cups granulated sugar
- ¼ cup light corn syrup
- ½ cup milk
- 1 stick or ½ cup butter or margarine
- 2 squares (1 ounce each) unsweetened chocolate, cut up
- ¼ teaspoon salt
- 1 teaspoon vanilla extract
- ¼ to ½ cup sifted confectioners' sugar (optional)

1. In a saucepan, combine the granulated sugar, corn syrup, milk, margarine, chocolate, and salt. Stir over low heat until the chocolate and margarine are melted. Bring to a full boil, stirring constantly. Boil for 1 minute or until the mixture reaches 220° on a candy thermometer.

2. Remove the saucepan from the heat. Beat the frosting with an electric mixer until the temperature drops to 120°, about 10 minutes of beating. Stir in the vanilla. Then continue beating until the frosting is cooled and smooth and has a good spreading consistency, about another 5 minutes. This frosting thickens as it stands. For a really stiff frosting, stir in the confectioners' sugar.

Your kitchen is a lab, so be a jolly mad scientist and experiment. That's how I came up with touches that make dishes more flavorful, such as adding a package of onion soup mix to cook a roast. Remember that recipes are just guidelines.

Larger than Life

Because we're blowin' in all directions like the four winds, we sometimes have to celebrate birthdays on the road. For Ashley's birthday this year, since she was auditioning in L.A., we joined her for a small family party by the hotel pool. Wy and the kids had just come from hanging out with Rosie O'Donnell, Larry joined us from Nashville, and I flew in from Knoxville, Tennessee, after a lecture. Ashley's oldest friend Gabby and her family rounded out the cozy group. The following day we had a private screening of Ashley's movie *Kiss the Girls* at Paramount Studios in Hollywood. It stars Ashley and Morgan Freeman and it's a thriller diller! As I was watching her on the big screen, the memory of all of Ashley's twenty-eight previous birthdays flashed before me. It was surreal!

Life Is Too Serious to Be Taken Seriously

Imagine this: You come in from work (Wy had been in the studio) and suddenly a helicopter lands in your backyard. Your hubby says he's taking you for a ride since it's your birthday. Next thing you know, you're setting down at Playland, an amusement center where all your family and friends are waiting to surprise you. Clowns greet you as you get out of the helicopter, while award-winning country group Sawyer Brown entertains onstage. Friends like Billy Dean, Michael McDonald (The Doobie Brothers), and David Pack (Ambrosia), take turns performing. All evening, friends kept coming up asking where to find Wy. "She's moved from Roller Blading to miniature golf to go-carts," I'd inform them. Wy, who's a kid at heart and very competitive, had sent someone ahead to test-drive the go-carts to find out which one was fastest before she went to race her buddies. It was the red one.

The littlest party girl: Grace, age one

Gotcha good, girl!

Eat Out More Often

Outside, that is—in the backyard, or even better at a park, a lake, a mountain, or the ocean. I couldn't afford to take my kids to restaurants. We were so poor, we went to KFC and licked other people's fingers. But Wy and Ashley had lots of fun at our picnics. One of the nicest things you can do for your family and friends is to learn the Heimlich Maneuver and C.P.R. Call your local Red Cross chapter.

How High Can You Jump?

After seeing the following gag on "America's Funniest Home Videos," I built a plywood box about 3 feet long and 1½ feet tall. It had small holes in the top and was screened on one end. After preparing a guest with a cock-and-bull story that we'd trapped a vicious mongoose, we let our visitor peer through the screen at a brown-and-gray furry critter with a tail. Then I opened the spring-loaded top so the coonskin cap flew up and hit the surprised victim in the chest.

For birthday parties, we cut a big hole through the top of a card table that was covered with a floor-length tablecloth. Over the hole we placed a large gift box with the bottom removed, and the lid gift-wrapped separately. Guests placed their real presents all around the empty box. A conspirator in a gorilla mask hunkered under the table and jumped up as the birthday person lifted off the lid to the fake box. When I pulled this on my friend Laurie, all the folks standing around the table were as startled as she. Laurie says it's the best gift she's ever gotten, and the best she's ever been gotten.

The art of living:
Not merely to look but see,
not just listen but hear,
not just experience but enjoy.

Celebrate Your Friends

The baby boomers hit fifty years old last year. We need to revise our image of growing older in this country. Among the biggest treasures in my life are my rockin' baby-boomer female friends.

Dr. Joan Borysenko is one of the most enlightened women on the planet! If you want to see for yourself, just pick up her latest book, *A Woman's Book of Life: The Biology, Psychology, and Spirituality of the Feminine Life Cycle*. It's about the connection between women's bodies, emotions, and spirit. Joan came to stay for a weekend at my farm and we were relaxing by the lake. As we discussed marriage, she had this insight: "I think intimacy is all about 'into me you see.'" This Ph.D. from Harvard is a cancer biologist, a prolific author, a yoga and meditation instructor, a wife, and a mother of three. Oh yeah, she's also a licensed psychologist. I've always said us women are each other's psychologists.

Another role model for all of us is Dr. Gladys McGarey, who has been a family physician for over fifty years and has just written her first book, called *The Physician Within*. Dr. Gladys, who is in her seventies, has dedicated her life to expanding the knowledge and application of holistic medical principles and advocating natural birthing.

But her greatest accomplishment is six kids who are in the fields of surgery, ministry, physical therapy, and counseling. I tell Dr. Gladys I want to be just like her when I grow up.

Life is a menu, and I'm always hungry.

Weddings and Anniversaries

When Larry and I were married in the spring of 1989, we suggested friends donate to a tree fund instead of buying gifts. Now there are flowering dogwoods and redbuds by our stone bridge as growing reminders of our love and our friends. On our anniversary, Larry and I share time alone. We may just walk in the valley and spend a quiet evening at home. We don't do discos. The best anniversary gift I ever received was when Larry bought himself a snore guard. It has allowed us to have a long and happy marriage.

Do you agree with this recent Roper Organization Survey on the five qualities women value most in a satisfying marriage? (1) Mutual love (2) Respect (3) Friendship (4) Shared values (5) Sexual satisfaction.

The best wedding trick I have ever pulled was when one of our crew guys got married. I had everybody in the Judd organization wrap up their own toaster and set it on the gift table at the reception. Meanwhile, in a back room, we assembled all the new gifts. As the happy bride opened the first toaster, she exclaimed, "Oh, how traditional! Every new bride needs a new toaster!" When the second one was a toaster, she politely said, "Well, when the first one breaks, because I know we'll have a long and happy marriage, we'll have a replacement." All of a sudden, she glanced over her shoulder and realized that every single package on the table was the same size! When everyone broke out in squeals of laughter, she got it!

People call me Cinderella because of my rags-to-riches story. Guess that makes Larry Prince Charming.

Curry Mayonnaise

My Mom makes this for special events. When thirty-some members of the church choir came over to the house, this would be on the relish platter. Here are some other places to try it: Dab a little on Wy's Cherry Jell-O Salad (page 31), or spread on chicken or roast beef sandwiches, or serve with a platter of fresh vegetables—carrot sticks, broccoli and cauliflower flowerets, red bell pepper strips, and other crunchy vegetables for dipping. This mayonnaise keeps well in the refrigerator, covered, for a week or two. Great for crowds.

MAKES ABOUT 2 CUPS

> 2 cups mayonnaise or mayonnaise-like salad dressing, regular, reduced-fat, or nonfat
> 2 teaspoons curry powder
> 2 teaspoons fresh lemon juice
> 2 teaspoons minced onion
> 2 teaspoons sweet pickle juice

In a small bowl, mix together all the ingredients. Cover and refrigerate for up to 2 weeks.

Attend class reunions.
It helps you remember who
you are and is a lot of fun.
And don't try to top others'
stories. If you want to really
make a good impression,
be attentive and excited for
their happiness.

Reunions

"Re-union" is to re-unify or come back to our origins. We feel it is so important to have contact with our family as a group once a year that we've begun having reunions at our farm every summer. One year it is the Strickland clan, and the next it is the Judd gang. It's of primary importance for us to connect with each other as evolving individuals and share our lives down through the years. Too often, families drift apart and all they have are frozen mental snapshots of images from the past. They tend to remember each other as the "bad little girl" or the "distant little boy" based on a single event from childhood. Why do we diligently put together photo albums if we don't share them? We love to bring ours out along with videos to have some laughs and reminisce. Everyone takes new pictures at each reunion and then makes reprints to share to keep us current in each other's minds while we're apart. I put my favorites on the insides of cabinet doors, so when I open my bedroom closet or kitchen cupboard the faces of my dear ones are smiling at me.

Every year something special seems to "fall from the sky." Last summer Calvin Lehew, a good-humored neighbor who builds and flies ultra-light planes, razzed our backyard while we were saddling up horses. When Calvin began dropping treats and dollar bills for the kids, my disbelieving nephew Josh began racing around with outstretched arms, exclaiming, "It's raining money!"

Three-Bean Salad

This recipe was given to my Mom by Sue Rice, the organist at the First Baptist Church in Ashland, Kentucky. You can substitute balsamic vinegar for part of the cider vinegar—experiment to suit your own taste. Robins, daffodils, and this salad always meant spring is on the way. It's a great addition to reunions or picnics.

MAKES 4 TO 6 SERVINGS

1 can (14½ ounces) cut green beans
1 can (14½ ounces) yellow wax beans
1 can (14½ ounces) kidney beans
½ cup minced green bell pepper
½ cup minced onion

DRESSING
¾ cup sugar
½ cup vegetable oil
½ cup cider vinegar
½ teaspoon salt
½ teaspoon black pepper

1. Drain and rinse all the beans. Let drain well. In a large bowl, combine the beans, bell pepper, and onion.

2. *Make the dressing:* In a glass jar with a screw top, combine the dressing ingredients and shake well to blend. Pour over the bean mixture and toss to mix well. Cover and refrigerate for up a day. To serve, let come to room temperature so the oil in the dressing will liquefy.

To Each His or Her Own

For our reunions, we have a plan of activities so that each one of us gets to do something we particularly enjoy. Mark likes to go hear bluegrass music at the Ryman Auditorium, and Margaret enjoys rowing on the lake. Mom hits the antique stores, and Jamie rides the four-wheeler. Allie loves to play badminton, and Josh likes to fish. Middy likes to ride in our old-fashioned horse-drawn Amish buggy. Brian gets to play in a life-size Indian tepee. Larry takes the kids in the back of a truck through the woods at night. Wy and Ashley enjoy twilight picnics down by the lake. Elijah is fascinated by playing down in our tornado cellar. My favorite part of the week is relaxing in the backyard in lawn chairs in the evening, full as a tick from a good supper and just being family.

Tool Time

My sister Margaret is a great cook, wife, mother, and homemaker, not to mention being my best friend and the all-time Trivial Pursuit champ. Here's two of her recipes. When she was giving them to me on the phone, and I asked what she had been doing, she casually replied, "Oh, just taking the door off Allison's room." Seems my darling eleven-year-old niece Allison, who had been sent to her room, decided to retaliate by continually banging her bedroom door. Margaret calmly warned her that having her own room and privacy was a privilege and she should stop. Sis is right handy with her set of Black & Decker tools. Allison now has some new tools for her psychological toolbox.

Nephews Brian and Josh and niece Allison would rather be active outdoors than at Disneyland.

Parmesan-Crusted Lemon Chicken

MAKES 4 SERVINGS

4 boneless, skinned chicken breast halves
5 tablespoons fresh lemon juice
2 eggs
1¼ cups dry bread crumbs
½ cup grated Parmesan cheese
2 teaspoons grated lemon peel
Salt and pepper to taste
3 tablespoons butter

1. Between 2 sheets of waxed paper, pound each chicken breast to ½ inch thickness. Place in a single layer in a baking dish. Pour 4 tablespoons of the lemon juice over the chicken and turn to coat. Let stand for 10 minutes.

2. In a small bowl, beat the eggs with the remaining 1 tablespoon lemon juice. In a shallow dish, combine the bread crumbs, Parmesan, and lemon peel.

3. Dip each chicken breast first into the egg mixture, then the crumb mixture to cover. Season with salt and pepper. Place on a sheet of waxed paper.

4. In a large, heavy, nonstick skillet, melt 2 tablespoons of the butter. Add half of the chicken and sauté until browned and cooked through, about 2 minutes per side. Remove to a platter and keep warm. Repeat with the remaining chicken and butter.

Zucchini and Squash Horseshoes

MAKES 4 SERVINGS

3 zucchini
1 yellow squash
2 tablespoons olive oil
1 clove garlic, minced
1 tomato, peeled, seeded, and chopped
1 teaspoon dried oregano
Salt and pepper to taste

1. Cut zucchini and squash in half lengthwise. Cut out the center seeded area or use a spoon to scoop it out. Cut into ¼-inch-thick slices to make horseshoe shapes.

2. In a large skillet, heat the oil over medium heat. Add the garlic and cook, stirring, until fragrant, about 30 seconds. Add the zucchini and squash and cook, stirring occasionally, until tender, about 5 minutes. Stir in the tomato and oregano. Simmer for about 2 minutes, and salt and pepper to taste.

It's All Relative

"If it ain't one thing, it's your mother," say Wy and Ashley.

The family surprised me to celebrate my good news, just as they stood by me when I'd gotten my bad news.

Although there's no cure yet for hepatitis C, an antiviral drug called Interferon may slow reproduction of the virus. After being on it for a year and experiencing very unpleasant side effects, I was thrilled to be taking my last shot. I was even more elated when a liver biopsy showed I was in remission! Wy and Ashley believe in celebrating such wonderful blessings and surprised me by having our whole family show up at the farm. I'm grateful to God, who's the Great Physician, and to my family and friends, who are my medicine.

The curative powers of faith, support, and positive thinking have been well documented. I'm living proof. Kahlil Gibran the poet wrote: "You pray in your distress and in your need: would that you might pray also in the fullness of your joy and in your days of abundance."

Celebrate family.

Well, thanks for visiting my kitchen.
You're always welcome
and valued here.
The door is always open
and my mind is never closed.

Mom and I enjoying a quiet moment
at my kitchen table

Metric Conversions

Weight equivalents

The metric weights given in this chart are not exact equivalents, but have been rounded up or down slightly to make measuring easier.

Avoirdupois	Metric
¼ oz	7 g
½ oz	15 g
1 oz	30 g
2 oz	60 g
3 oz	90 g
4 oz	115 g
5 oz	150 g
6 oz	175 g
7 oz	200 g
8 oz (½ lb)	225 g
9 oz	250 g
10 oz	300 g
11 oz	325 g
12 oz	350 g
13 oz	375 g
14 oz	400 g
15 oz	425 g
16 oz (1 lb)	450 g
1 lb 2 oz	500 g
1½ lb	750 g
2 lb	900 g
2¼ lb	1 kg
3 lb	1.4 kg
4 lb	1.8 kg
4½ lb	2 kg

Volume equivalents

These are not exact equivalents for the American cups and spoons, but have been rounded up or down slightly to make measuring easier.

American	Metric	Imperial
¼ t	1.25 ml	
½ t	2.5 ml	
1 t	5 ml	
½ T (1½ t)	7.5 ml	
1 T (3 t)	15 ml	
¼ cup (4 T)	60 ml	2 fl oz
⅓ cup (5 T)	75 ml	2½ fl oz
½ cup (8 T)	125 ml	4 fl oz
⅔ cup (10 T)	150 ml	5 fl oz (¼ pint)
¾ cup (12 T)	175 ml	6 fl oz (⅓ pint)
1 cup (16 T)	250 ml	8 fl oz
1¼ cups	300 ml	10 fl oz (½ pint)
1½ cups	350 ml	12 fl oz
1 pint (2 cups)	500 ml	16 fl oz
2½ cups	625 ml	20 fl oz (1 pint)
1 quart (4 cups)	1 litre	1¾ pints

Oven Temperature equivalents

Oven	°F.	°C.	Gas Mark
very cool	250–275	130–140	½–1
cool	300	150	2
warm	325	170	3
moderate	350	180	4
moderately hot	375	190	5
	400	200	6
hot	425	220	7
very hot	450	230	8
	475	250	9

John Grisham, the best-selling novelist, once told me, "The book is always better than the movie."

Bibliography

Newsletters

Christiane Northrup's Health Wisdom for Women Newsletter

Dr. Andrew Weil Self-Healing Newsletter, Thorne Communications, Watertown, Massachusetts

Healthy Bites Newsletter, Hope Publications, Hope Heart Institute, Seattle, Washington

Noetic Sciences Review, Institute of Noetic Sciences, Sausalito, California

Psychology and Health Update Newsletter, Business Concepts, Inc., Santa Barbara, California

Books

Acts of Faith: Daily Meditation for People of Color, by Iyanla Vanzant (Fireside Books, Simon and Schuster, New York © 1993)

The Bible

The Book of Questions, by Gregory Stock, Ph.D., (Workman Publishing, New York © 1987)

David Letterman's New Book of Top Ten Lists and Wedding Dress Patterns for the Husky Bride, by David Letterman and the Late Show with David Letterman Writers (Bantam Books, New York © 1996)

Handbook for the Soul, by Richard Carlson and Benjamin Shield (Little Brown and Company, Boston, Massachusetts © 1995)

A House Blessing, by Welleran Poltarness (Blue Lantern Books © 1994)

If It's Going To Be It's Up To Me, by Robert H. Schuller (Harper San Francisco © 1997)

Kitchen Table Wisdom: Stories That Heal, by Rachel Naomi Remen (A Riverhead Book, Division of G.P. Putnam's Sons © 1996)

The Life We Are Given, by George Leonard and Michael Murphy (A Jeremy P. Tarcher/Putnam Book, G.P. Putnam's Sons, New York © 1995)

Managing Stress (Second Edition), by Brian Luke Seward (Jones and Bartlett Publishers, Sudbury, Massachusetts © 1997)

The Physician Within You, by Gladys Taylor McGarey, M.D., M.D.H. (Health Communications, Deerfield Beach, Florida © 1997)

Quotable Quotes, Reader's Digest © 1997

The Shelter of Each Other: Rebuilding Our Families, by Mary Pipher, Ph.D. (Ballantine Books, Division of Random House Inc., New York © 1996)

Simpler Times, by Thomas Kincade (Harvest House, Eugene, Oregon © 1996)

Teach Only Love, by Gerald G. Jampolsy, M.D. (Bantam Books, New York, Toronto © 1983)

A Woman's Book of Life, by Joan Borysenko, Ph.D. (A Riverhead Book, Division of G.P. Putnam's Sons, New York © 1996)

Photo Credits

All food photos by Steven Mark Needham

Kay Baber—page 52

Lesley Bohm—page 179

Joe Collins Photography, Dallas, TX—page 91

David Coyle—page 148

Henry Diltz—page 102

Slick Lawson—pages 9 and 167

Christopher Little—page 40

Alan L. Mayor—page 75

Theresa Montgomery: TNN—Pages iii and 209

Peter Nash—pages 45, 60, 74, 87, 94, and 118

Don Newton, Jr.—pages 44 and 47

Dewey Nicks—pages 14 (bottom)

Chip Powell—pages 1, 3, 43, 70, 71, 73, 81, 89, 92, 111, 121, 143, 149 (top), 158, and 195

Penny Webb—page 4

All other photos courtesy of Naomi Judd

Recipe Index